Making Cards and Invitations

APPLE

Sugar and spice and everything nice,
That's what our Sofia is made of!

Please help us wish our sweetie-pie
a happy third birthday.

Sunday, August 5
4:00 p.m.
58 State Street

rsvp: 752-555-2999

Alexis

EFA

be mine

Making Cards and Invitations

How to Design Personalised Stationery at Home

patty hoffman, megan eisen and josh eisen of mountaincow

Published in the UK in 2005 by
Apple Press
Sheridan House
112/116A Western Road
Hove BN3 1DD
UK

www.apple-press.com

ISBN 1-84543-009-3

10 9 8 7 6 5 4 3 2 1

Design: Yee Design
Cover Image: Annie Schlechter
Cover Design: Megan Eisen

Reference, page 100:
Baldrige, Letitia. *Letitia Baldrige's New Manners for New Times: A Complete Guide to Etiquette*. New
York: Scribner, 2003.
Feinberg, Steven L. *Crane's Blue Book of Stationery: The Styles and Etiquette of Letters, Notes and
Announcements*. New York: Doubleday, 1989.
Spade, Kate. *Manners*. New York: Simon & Schuster, 2004.

Reference, page 117:
Feinberg, Steven L. *Crane's Wedding Blue Book: The Styles and Etiquette of Announcements,
Invitations, and Other Correspondences*. New York: Simon & Schuster, 1993.
Post, Peggy. *Emily Post's Wedding Etiquette: Cherished Traditions and Contemporary Ideas for a
Joyous Celebration*. Fourth Edition. New York: HarperCollins, 2000.

Printed in Singapore

Photography

Annie Schlechter's photography has appeared in *Martha Stewart Living*, *Child*, and *New York* Magazine. Her team included stylist Laura Iler, whose work has appeared in magazines including *Martha Stewart Living*, *Real Simple*, *Fortune*, and *Redbook*, as well as catalogues for Bloomingdale's, Linens 'n Things and Macy's.

Acknowledgments

Patty, Megan and Josh greatly appreciate the many contributions from expert invitation designers, event planners and everyday hosts and hostesses, without whom this book would not be nearly so helpful and enjoyable. Thank you all so much for sharing your happy occasions and expertise with Mountaincow:

Peggy Andrews, Zoe Bachelor, Lauren Barnett, Allana Baroni, Zida Borcich, Chris Brahe, Kim Broggi, Erica Busch, Joan Buyce, Susan Burdick, Susan Cahoon, Andrea Crane, Jen DeGraphenreed, Judith Eisen, Deborah Fabricant, Sara Lippmann Feig, Stephanie Field, Jessica Graham, Kim Hammer, Lisa Hasbrook, Eva Hoffman, Sam Hoffman, Linda Kaye, Melinda Konopko, Jennifer Laduca, Erika Lenkert, Renda Marsh, Risa Meyer, Maureen Petrellese, Michelle Rago, Kathy Reuter, Teresa Rodgers, Ramon Ruiz, Justine Schembri, Sherry Schweitzer, Clay Siegert, Johanna Skier, Audrey Slater, Nancy Slotnick, Kate Wallace, Joshua Wesson and Wendy Zalinsky.

contents

FOR ALL SEASONS

FOR CELEBRATIONS AND SOIRÉES

FOR IN-BETWEEN PARTIES

TOOLS AND TECHNIQUES

introduction

WITH A HOUSEFUL OF KIDS AND A LARGE FAMILY, WE ARE ALWAYS celebrating birthdays, weddings, holidays, or new babies. We love to make every occasion special, but we don't always have the time to do everything by hand. However, that doesn't mean we can't still make a personal statement with our invitations. We wrote this book to show how easy and fun it can be to create invitations yourself using a computer and printer.

Megan has been making all our invitations and announcements for the last ten years with plain card stock and store-bought stationery on her computer. She found that she didn't have to spend a lot of money or order custom invitations from a book to get really fabulous, professional-looking results designed exactly the way she wanted.

When our second child was born, Megan knew the exact design she wanted for the announcement. However, since we had just moved to Rhode Island and hadn't even found a stationery store, we decided to order the announcements preprinted. No matter how hard we looked, we couldn't find exactly what we wanted, and we weren't willing to settle for less than perfect for our baby.

So once again, we made the announcement ourselves. The complexity of the announcement (faded photo edges, small card with vellum overlay, ribbon holes, and addressed envelopes) required a combination of several software applications to achieve the final piece. While struggling through it we looked at each other and said, "We could make this process so much easier!" And so our company, Mountaincow, was born.

We designed our flagship software program, PrintingPress, to make it easy to take any size paper or stationery and turn it into a beautiful custom invitation or announcement. We added a built-in address book with separate mailing lists for each project to make addressing envelopes a breeze. We even added some party-planning features, such as tracking RSVP count, guest list, and gifts received to make the process of throwing a party more organized.

Our customers never tire of new ideas for invitations. When we met Patty, we immediately knew that her abundant enthusiasm for stationery and her background writing for magazines made her the perfect person to help bring this book to life. Together, the three of us created this book using a series of elegant but easy-to-achieve project ideas for all occasions. We included a bonus CD with a selection of fonts and images to help you get started. We hope this book shows how easy it is to take simple elements and customize them to your needs to create the exact invitation you want.

Megan and Josh Eisen
Co-founders of Mountaincow

chapter 1

for the
bride & groom

breaking out of the mold

A Modern Wedding

When Peggy Andrews opened The Unique Bride in Burlingame, California, twenty years ago, she saw a number of brides planning destination weddings. "I'd say about five out of every hundred brides were getting married in Hawaii," Peggy says. "Now I see that tenfold. Brides are getting married in Hawaii, Montana, Mexico—all over." Peggy says they're planned like a southern-style wedding, where a series of events are held over four or five days.

"I just received six pieces of mail pertaining to just one wedding," says Peggy. "This couple is from New York City but is getting married in Vail, Colorado. Because different people are hosting the various events, I get multiple invitations," says Peggy. "The bride's grandmother invited me to the rehearsal dinner. Then I got something for all the fun things to do in Vail. Then the wedding invitations were printed with a design that looked like an evergreen to convey they were getting married in the mountains."

Destination weddings are just one way brides are stepping away from tradition. And, of course, invitations follow suit.

New York City wedding designer Michelle Rago urges her clients to be like the Vail bride and create what she calls site-specific invitations. "Invitations are the guests' first impression. They set the tone and give guests a sense of what kind of wedding it's going to be."

"I think you can have an extremely upscale, sophisticated affair and personalize it through whimsical touches that remind people of the couple. You can be nontraditional but still have it feel sophisticated and traditional," says Michelle.

One of Michelle's brides was getting married on a farm in Vermont. She found beautiful hand-sketched images of farm animals to use on the invitation and matched them to the escort card. "It was both sophisticated and fun."

"Couples want something different," says Zoe Bachelor, marketing director of Studio Z Mendocino stationery. "Even if it's coming out of a sample book of invitations, couples will opt for the orange design with blue writing."

Michelle agrees. "Brides are looking for a way to do something a little different from the seventeen other weddings they've attended that year."

Enter the modern invitation. Starring ... color.

"Brides are now using color to personalize their wedding," says Michelle. "They might try a red card with white writing. It's just reversing the obvious, but it's taking a leap."

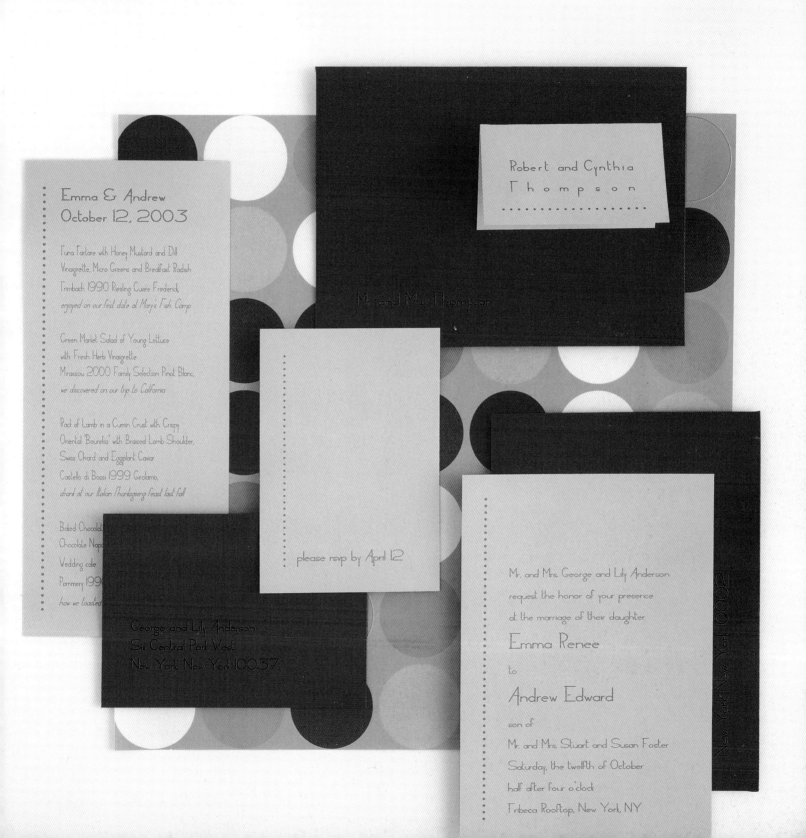

Emma & Andrew
October 12, 2003

Tuna Tartare with Honey Mustard and Dill
Vinaigrette, Micro Greens and Breakfast Radish
Trimbach 1990 Riesling Cuvee Frederick,
enjoyed on our first date at Mary's Fish Camp

Green Market Salad of Young Lettuce
with Fresh Herb Vinaigrette
Mirassou 2000 Family Selection Pinot Blanc,
we discovered on our trip to California

Rack of Lamb in a Cumin Crust with Crispy
Oriental 'Bourelia' with Braised Lamb Shoulder,
Swiss Chard and Eggplant Caviar
Castello di Bossi 1999 Girolamo,
drank at our Italian Thanksgiving feast last fall

Baked Chocolate
Chocolate Napo
Wedding cake
Pommery 1990
how we toasted

George and Lily Anderson
Six Central Park West
New York, New York 10037

Robert and Cynthia
Thompson
. . . .

Mr. and Mrs. Thompson

please rsvp by April 12

Mr. and Mrs. George and Lily Anderson
request the honor of your presence
at the marriage of their daughter

Emma Renee
to

Andrew Edward

son of
Mr. and Mrs. Stuart and Susan Foster
Saturday, the twelfth of October
half after four o'clock
Tribeca Rooftop, New York, NY

New York, New York 10002

GETTING STARTED

If you're leaning away from the traditional cream card with black script, the first thing to ask yourself is, What are you looking for? With endless fonts, graphics, and paper choices, this question can be overwhelming.

Start by defining the personality of your event. This aspect will affect all the following choices: color, paper, graphics, and elements you will include in your invitation.

FIND YOUR WEDDING'S PERSONALITY

Audrey and Bill were certain of only one thing when it came to their wedding: They wanted to be married on Shelter Island, a scenic beach located exactly between both their parents' homes in New York and Connecticut. Once they selected a date in late September, the rest of their wedding took shape. Fall on the North Shore of Long Island means rows and rows of sunflowers in top bloom and roadside farm stands selling bushels of apples. Using nature as their wedding planner, the sunflower became the subtle motif of their special day, and they decided to forgo a traditional wedding cake for fresh-baked apple pies.

"We wanted our wedding to be relaxed and pretty, above anything else," explains Audrey. "We didn't want anything to be formal; that's just not our personality. I didn't really do anything too different on the day of our wedding. I wasn't a princess-y bride—I was a beachy bride."

First, Audrey and Bill sent their guests hotel information on gold paper with an illustration of a sunflower. They suggested quaint bed and breakfasts, noteworthy restaurants, and guides for typical Shelter Island activities, from bird watching to antique shopping.

For their invitation, they used a more elaborate version of the sunflower illustration, which was repeated on every piece of stationery, including the response card and directions. When guests arrived at the hotel, the sunflower greeted them on a gift tag attached to lemon drop cookies from a local bakery.

"Weddings are all the same to some degree, and this was just our spin on it," says Audrey. "We had our place cards hanging from pegs, like the buddy board we used to have at camp. We just wanted everyone to be comfortable, like we were one big extended family."

Embracing an image is the perfect way to create the feeling you want for your wedding. Use the images included in PrintingPress, your own drawings, or graphics you've either bought or found free on the Internet. Add a consistent but ever-changing image by recoloring it every time you use it. One warning: Don't overuse graphics or your invitation will look less sophisticated. Choose one or two images you love and stick with them.

Another benefit: These images are easy to re-create on your favors, wedding website, and programs.

If you're using a photograph, make it more dramatic by changing its color to black and white or sepia tones. Photographs also make a terrific background image. Be sure the type you choose is easy to read on top of the photo. You may need to make the photo more transparent or the type darker or bolder.

If you'd like your project to be border-free, or "bleed" to the end of the page, you can trim your paper to the outline of the background photo. If you've used a black-and-white photo, this effect will give your project a vintage-postcard feel. If you choose a glossy paper, your project will be more like an actual photograph.

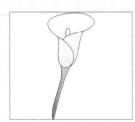

CHOOSING YOUR COLORS

You may have chosen your wedding colors at age ten, in which case, you are in good shape. Otherwise, outside circumstances may help dictate your colors. A couple who met while working in an ice cream parlor may want to choose the confection combination of brown, ivory, and pink, whereas a New York City bride with a "Big Apple" theme may want reds and silver. Think about your reception, the time of year you're getting married, or, more simply, your favorite color.

In the invitation shown, the harmonizing, warm colors of salmon and cranberry are tied together with modern, cranberry-colored type. It is important when choosing colors in the same family that adequate contrast exists between them or the information will be impossible to read. Shades of red are visually strong. Stay away from using light-colored ink, especially when printing large blocks of text. See Chapter Seven, "Tools & Techniques," for more information on color.

To make the most important information stand out, limit the number of colors you use to two or three. It's helpful to keep the color consistent with the type of information it displays. For instance, if the invitation is salmon and cranberry, the additional information for the hotels and directions can be printed on a coordinating lavender paper. This way, the invitation remains unique, and guests know to look for the lavender paper for secondary information.

"Don't force all the pieces of your invitation to be an exact match," advises Megan Eisen, CEO of Mountaincow, "Think coordinate, not match. Pair a dark blue envelope with a sky blue card. Or find a card that's a more intense shade of the envelope color. The invitation will really pop when your guests open it."

	COLOR	WHAT IT MEANS	BEST FOR
	BLUE	EARTHY, CALM	BEACH WEDDING
	GREEN	HEALING, SPRING	GARDEN WEDDING
	RED	POWER	BLACK TIE
	PINK	SOFT, FEMININE	ROMANTIC
	YELLOW	PEACE	SMALL, AFTERNOON WEDDING
	PURPLE	REGAL	CHURCH WEDDING

SELECTING PAPER

Before purchasing any paper, know what type of printer you plan to use to print your invitations. If you're using an ink-jet printer and are not sure if a certain paper will work, ask for a few sample sheets before committing to an entire batch. If you don't live near a stationery store with a wide variety of paper, it's worth it to make a special trip to one. Ask for some sample sheets, and then place your order later, after you've tested your samples.

How much you want to spend on your invitations will influence your choice of paper. Some stationery and office supply stores sell kits with coordinating paper and envelopes. Buying a ream of standard letter-size card stock allows you to create unique shapes such as elongated rectangles and rounded corners using a rotary paper cutter and punches. (See Chapter Seven, "Tools & Techniques," for more information on tools.) Depending on the complexity of your design, you might want to have your paper cut professionally to save time and to avoid mistakes.

While you're shopping, be sure to keep the envelopes in mind because their variety is usually more limited. Custom-size envelopes are often expensive and available only in large quantities.

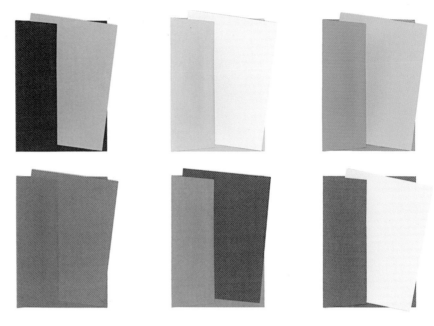

"Think coordinate, not match."

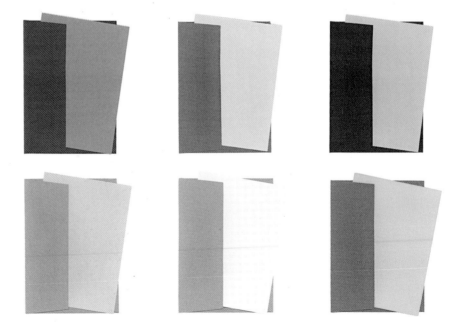

TYPEFACE

The typeface you choose can dramatically affect the style your invitation communicates. First and foremost, it must be easy to read. Second, the font you select should tell the same story as the color and paper choices you've made so far.

IF YOU WANT	USE	
CAREFREE	THIN LETTERING, SANS SERIF	*Alexis is turning one!*
SERIOUS	SIMPLE SERIF, POSSIBLY SMALL CAPS	Please join us for dinner
ROMANTIC	FLOURISHED SCRIPT	*at the marriage of their daughter*
INFORMAL	HANDWRITING-LIKE	Frank's 40th Fiesta!

Limit the number of fonts you use to one or two. Zida Borcich, designer of Studio Z Mendocino Stationery explains, "Too many typefaces looks like a hodge-podge. Use the bold, italic, and bold italic font styles to create different textures without using a second or third typeface. If you use too many typefaces, you risk making your invitation look amateurish and illegible. If you think something looks funny, it probably does."

Megan prefers adding emphasis using a contrasting font rather than using bold or italic. "I sometimes use a script font just for the names of the bride and groom—they'll stand out in a good way."

In this modern wedding invitation, only *Beckles Wide* is used, and it's anything but boring. The names of the bride and groom were made larger on the invitation card, the font was made smaller on the reply card, and the guest names were fully justified on the place card. The result is a clean, beautiful invitation.

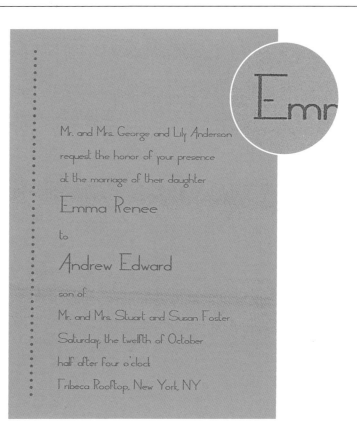

Mr. and Mrs. George and Lily Anderson
request the honor of your presence
at the marriage of their daughter
Emma Renee
to
Andrew Edward
son of
Mr. and Mrs. Stuart and Susan Foster
Saturday, the twelfth of October
half after four o'clock
Tribeca Rooftop, New York, NY

SPECIAL TOUCHES

Vellum, grommets, ribbon, or twine can add a unique element to your invitation. By using PrintingPress's ribbon hole markers, you can produce flawless, multilayered invitations. To really make something stand out, print it on a small card and attach it with a ribbon to a larger card.

Our wedding weekend

Lucy & Charles
July 4-6, 2004

Welcome

Things to do

Important Phone Numbers

Schedule of Events

Directions

WHAT TO SAY

"The words you choose are important when creating invitations," says Erika Lenkert, author of *The Last-Minute Party Girl: Fashionable, Fearless and Foolishly Simple Entertaining.* "First and foremost, an invitation is informational. Keep it short and easy to read."

It may seem obvious that you need to include the names of the bride and groom and both of their parents and stepparents, but the consequence of any omission makes it worth checking these names twice. Also be sure to include the wedding date and time, and the names and addresses of the ceremony and reception sites.

Information pertaining to attire or rain date varies on an individual basis. Special instructions for children or gifts may also be included in special circumstances. Often couples marrying for a second time will request no gifts or ask that donations be made in their honor to a specific cause. Consult an etiquette book or a friend whose opinion you trust for the wording of such requests.

For more information on the wording of invitations, see Chapter Seven.

Basic formula

Invitational line
Request line
Bride's name
Joining word
Groom's name
Date line
Year line
Time line
Location
City, State

PICK OUT THE PIECES

Despite its modern design, this wedding invitation has all the traditional pieces: an invitation card, a response card, a self-addressed stamped envelope, and both inner and outer envelopes. A place card and menu are also designed to coordinate with the invitation.

"I recommend inner and outer envelopes and response cards," says Michelle. "For my wedding, I didn't do a response card because I wanted people to respond to me on their own stationery. I ended up having to call more people than I expected. Now I recommend a response card with an obvious space for people to write a note."

Zoe, however, feels inner envelopes are optional. "We no longer have a footman delivering invitations by horse and carriage. There isn't a need for an inner envelope to be set on the butler's silver tray."

Invitation

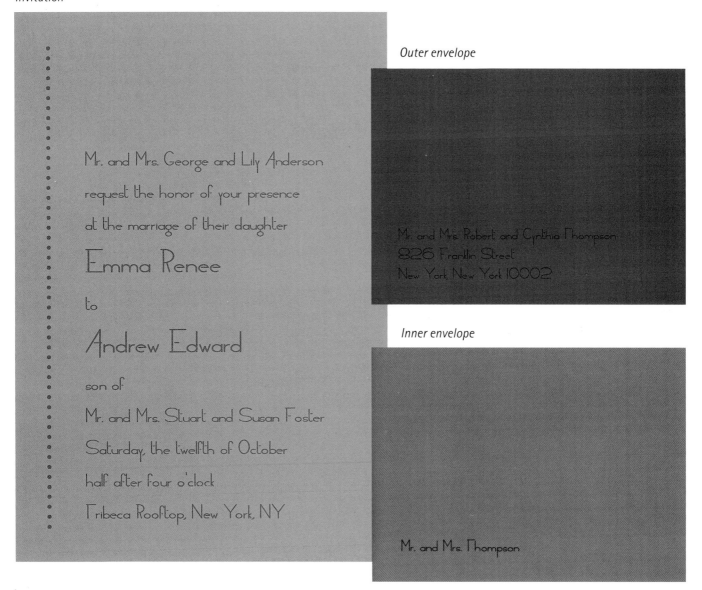

Mr. and Mrs. George and Lily Anderson

request the honor of your presence

at the marriage of their daughter

Emma Renee

to

Andrew Edward

son of

Mr. and Mrs. Stuart and Susan Foster

Saturday, the twelfth of October

half after four o'clock

Tribeca Rooftop, New York, NY

Outer envelope

Mr. and Mrs. Robert and Cynthia Thompson
826 Franklin Street
New York, New York 10002

Inner envelope

Mr. and Mrs. Thompson

Unless your reception is buffet-style, you'll need escort cards with your guests' names and assigned table numbers. If you wish to assign each seat, you can also make coordinating place cards for the tables. Because place cards and escort cards are small, shy away from overly ornate fonts, but don't compensate with tiny lettering, either.

A menu card is an important element if you're offering your guests a choice of entrees. It's also another chance to personalize your wedding. In this example, the couple has put a lot of thought into the selection of the wines they are serving. They've explained the significance of each choice in italic under the course.

The Project

Now that you've carefully chosen the color, paper, font, and wording, you can start making your modern wedding invitation project.

In this example, a repeated dot graphic is used on the longest side of the paper to tie all the pieces together. To do this on the invitation, menu, and response card, make the text margins larger on the left and find a border or line pattern you love and insert it there.

The invitation shown is 5" x 7" (12.7 x 17.8 cm) with a left margin of 1" (2.5 cm). The response card is 3½" x 5" (8.9 x 12.7 cm) and the menu is 4" x 9" (10.2 x 22.9 cm), both of which have a ½" (1.9 cm) left margin.

The place card is 3½" x 4" (8.9 x 12.7 cm) with a horizontal fold. The text is fully justified, meaning it is aligned on both the right and left edges. See Chapter Seven, "Tools & Techniques," for more information on text justification. The dots on the place card have been inserted to run along the bottom, under the guest's name.

In this project, the same font was used on the envelopes and the invitation. The names and addresses were placed on the far-left side to complement the design of the other pieces.

See Chapter Seven, "Tools & Techniques," for more information on printing inner and outer envelopes.

Escort card (outside)

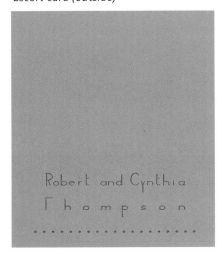

Robert and Cynthia
Thompson

Escort card (inside)

Table Eight

Menu

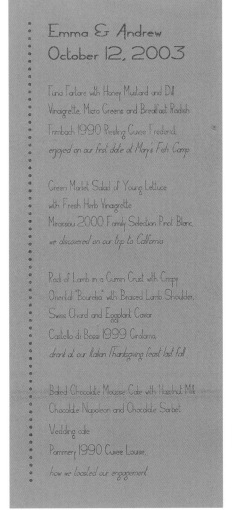

Emma & Andrew
October 12, 2003

Tuna Tartare with Honey Mustard and Dill
Vinaigrette, Micro Greens and Breakfast Radish
Trimbach 1990 Riesling Cuvee Frederic
enjoyed on our first date at Mary's Fish Camp

Green Market Salad of Young Lettuce
with Fresh Herb Vinaigrette
Mirassou 2000 Family Selection Pinot Blanc
we discovered on our trip to California

Rack of Lamb in a Cumin Crust with Crispy
Oriental "Bouretia" with Braised Lamb Shoulder,
Swiss Chard and Eggplant Caviar
Castello di Bossi 1999 Girolamo,
drank at our Italian Thanksgiving feast last fall

Baked Chocolate Mousse Cake with Hazelnut Milk
Chocolate Napoleon and Chocolate Sorbet
Wedding cake
Pommery 1990 Cuvee Louise,
how we toasted our engagement

Mr. and Mrs. Thompson

Mr. and Mrs. George and Lily Anderson

request the honor of your presence

at the marriage of their daughter

Emma Renee

to

Andrew Edward

son of

Mr. and Mrs. Stuart and Susan Foster

Saturday, the twelfth of October

half after four o'clock

Tribeca Rooftop New York, NY

George and Lily Anderson
416 Chamb...
New York...

The favor of a reply is requested
before the first of September

M _____

will _____ attend

Mr. and Mrs. Robert and Cynthia
Thompson

Mr. and Mrs. Robert and Cynthia
826 Franklin Street
New York, New York 100

here comes the bride

Nice Day for a White Wedding

"Every time I see letterpress printing, it brings me back to 1456," says Zida Borcich, a designer at Studio Z Mendocino, referring to the Gutenberg Bible, the first book printed with moveable type. Letterpress is a process in which plates of raised type are pressed into paper and leave an imprint you can both see and feel. "When I see beautiful printing on fluffy paper with deep impressions, I also see the long history of beauty and I know it was in the hands of an artist."

Even to an untrained eye, letterpress conveys a special, important event. "A wedding invitation that carries the weight and beauty of letterpress says 'get ready for love,'" Zida explains.

So why aren't all wedding invitations printed in letterpress? "The cost can be prohibitive," explains Zida. Luckily, companies such as Studio Z make stationery with letterpressed designs that can be fed into a home printer, so anyone can afford the elegance of letterpress.

A BEAUTIFUL HYBRID

"I love the idea of marrying this ancient craft to this new technology," says Zida. "To have letterpress cards and be able to print them at home is fantastic."

Zida offers many tips on how to make the combination work. "Proportion is very important," she says. "Look closely at the letterpress design and start from there. If the design is in the center, center your text. If you have a delicate image, do not use a big, fat sans serif."

The invitation isn't the only place you can make combined styles work together. If your budget doesn't allow for a letterpress wedding program, Zida suggests doing just the cover in letterpress. "Use your printer for the inside pages. This way you can add photographs, too," she says.

A FORMAL AFFAIR

Just as a letterpress invitation conveys the importance of an event, the style of a wedding invitation speaks volumes about the wedding. A formal invitation, usually on a white or ecru card with black lettering, will most likely call for a church wedding, as opposed to an informal lunch wedding at the bride and groom's home. Even more formal is a folded card with text only on the front flap.

The pieces you choose to include in the envelope will also give clues to the type of event you are planning. Using outer and inner envelopes, a tradition from the days when invitations were delivered on horseback, and tissue paper, once used to blot ink, are both traditional gestures.

Whether your wedding will have your guests in tuxedos and gowns or khakis and sundresses, you must include following information on a traditional wedding invitation:

- **Return address.** *The back flap of the envelope provides the most elegant placement for a return address, keeping the front of the envelope uncluttered. It also lets the invitation stand out from the bills and everyday mail.*

- **Reception card.** *If the wedding reception will take place in a different location from the ceremony, or there is a different guest list for the celebration, a small reception card with the name and address of the reception site must be added.*

- **Response card and envelope.** *A small card and pre-addressed, stamped envelope is essential for ensuring responses to your invitation. This can be a blank card with a preferred date for a response, or it can have a line for your guests to fill in their name. Believe it or not, many people forget to write their names when responding. It's a good idea to write a small code number on the back of the reply cards in case this happens.*

- **Map and directions.** *These are not mandatory, but providing them is a nice service for your guests. If your reception hall does not supply a map or directions, use an Internet map search to create one. Be sure to test the directions to make sure any road changes have been included.*

- **Print more than you need.** *It's a good idea to print at least ten extra invitations. Doing so prevents you from not having the right paper when you need a last-minute invitation, and you will have some for a keepsake.*

- **Extra envelopes.** *To be safe, buy an extra twenty-five envelopes. Flaws in the paper, spills, and other mess-ups are bound to happen.*

WATCH YOUR LANGUAGE

Decide early on what style of wording you prefer and stay consistent. Many sources are available to help you compose an invitation and guide you through the options of spellings and proper etiquette for practically any family situation. Divorces, second marriages, titles, military rank, who is throwing the wedding, and the mixing of religions can complicate the process. Check the Internet or a bookstore for a source and find a style that you like—then embrace it. You will be using this style not only for the invitation and addressing the envelopes but also for the place cards and thank-you notes.

STUFF IT

When it's time to collate your various enclosures, create a pile with each piece facing up. Start with the invitation at the bottom. If you are including tissue paper, place it on top of the invitation. Next, add the reception card, then the map card. Tuck the response card face up under the flap of the response envelope, and place them both on top of the pile so that the response card is on top. Place the pile in the inner envelope with the printed side facing up. Then turn the inner envelope over and insert it into the outer envelope with the names of the guests facing up.

Keeping a consistent tone, the place card used the same proper titles of the guests as the outer envelope. The inside of the place card reads formally, You are seated at Table Eight.

The response card is 5" x 3½" (12.7 x 8.9 cm), a standard size known as "4-bar," with a top margin of 1⅛" (2.9 cm). The request for the reply is consistent with the formal wording of the invitation and uses the American spelling of favor. (The invitation used the American spelling of honor.)

The Project

The invitation, reply card, coordinating envelopes, and place card were printed on Studio Z Mendocino's Lily collection of gold-foil letterpress stationery. The first consideration when using preprinted stationery is to determine the margins around the design. Use a clear ruler to measure the spacing of the design on the card.

For the 5" x 7" (12.7 x 17.7 cm) invitation, make the top margin $1\frac{1}{2}$" (3.8 cm) to create an even white space from the top of the card to the top of the text. Following Zida's advice, the font used is both centered and delicate to complement the letterpress dragonfly. The bride and groom's names stand out on their individual lines. The wording uses formal titles and phrases, such as request the honor of your presence, connoting a formal event.

Invitation

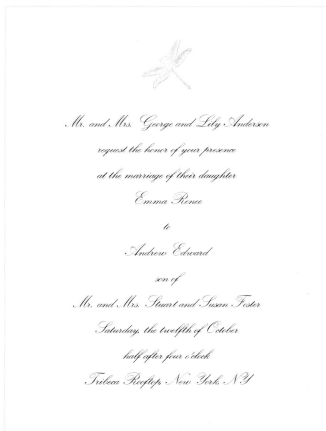

The inner envelope, an A7 with a gold-foil letterpress dragonfly, simply used the titles of the guests without their first names. The outer envelope, an A8, used titles and both of their first names and address.

Inner envelope

Outer envelope

mark your calendar

Engaging News

Save-the-date cards have always been used by couples who plan a destination wedding, are getting married on a holiday weekend, or have many guests coming in from out of town who need to make travel plans. However, more and more couples are deciding to send save-the-date cards to their entire guest list as early as a year in advance.

 "Our wedding was only a short drive to the beach from where we live," says Eva Hoffman, a New York bride. "And even though it wasn't technically the busy season, we wanted to make sure our guests had first dibs at the great B&Bs and quaint hotels out there. Because so many places had two-night minimum stays, our guests needed time to plan a fun weekend around our wedding."

LICENSE TO HAVE FUN

"You can be creative with a save-the-date card," says Megan. "Wedding invitations can be so formal, but here's an opportunity to have fun, show your personalities, or introduce a style concept."

"We were married on the Fourth of July, so we used a photograph my husband took of an American flag," says Sara Lippmann Feig, a writer from Philadelphia whose husband, Rob, is an avid photographer. "Inside we wrote: It may be Independence Day, but we're getting married! We had fun with it. But when it came to the actual invitations, we chose traditional ivory cards."

GIVE THE SCOOP

"Your save-the-date card should have as much information about your wedding as you know at the time," says Megan.

"Obviously, the single most important piece of information on the card is when your wedding is taking place. If you know where you're getting married, include that as well. You should also indicate that a formal invitation will follow."

Travel information is essential for destination weddings, especially if the locale requires special arrangements such as taking a ferry or flying into a small airport with few flights.

For Clay Siegert, a board game designer from Boston, planning a wedding in Nantucket led to an information-packed save-the-date card. "We chose a trifold card so we could include as much information as possible about the wedding weekend for our guests. Because we have friends and family coming from all over the country, we knew they would appreciate having as much information about the wedding and Nantucket as possible," says Clay.

"On the save-the-date cards we included the usual wedding day schedule information, as well as information about different hotel options, airlines that serve the island, and ferry information. On the cards, we also listed our wedding website, which contains even more information, such as maps and photos. On the site we also wrote fun bios about ourselves and the people in our wedding party."

Often, if you arrange a room block with a hotel, they will provide preprinted cards with their reservation information and directions. "You can send these cards along with your save-the-date card in the same envelope," says Megan. "This way you can keep the beauty of the card you

Save the date to celebrate the wedding of
Emma Anderson and Andrew Foster
Saturday, May 1, 2004
The Newport Inn, Newport, RI
Invitation to follow

Robert and Cynthia Thompson
826 Franklin Street
New York, New York 10002

Please join us for a
bridal shower honoring

Emma Anderson

Saturday, February 28
2 o'clock
Main Street
Larchmont, NY

Megan was starry-eyed
when they met

Josh won her heart

They fell in love

They're getting married!
December 12, 2004
Save the date!

Invitation to follow

Here's the scoop:

Patty and Chris
are getting married
Sunday October 10, 2004

Fiddler's Elbow
Bedminster, NJ

Invitation and details to follow.
Please save the date!

designed without cluttering it with all of the hotel's information about rates and check-out times."

SIGN, SEAL, DELIVER

Save-the-date cards can be sent as early as a year in advance of the wedding or as late as six months in advance. "It's really never too early if you know the date and place," says Megan. "Everyone with a packed schedule will appreciate the advance notice."

WHO NEEDS IT?

Anyone who receives a save-the-date card must be invited to the wedding. "There is no back-pedaling here," says Megan. "Work with your final 'A' list when creating the mailing list for your save-the-date cards. Keep in mind that people know each other and will assume the worst if a friend receives a save-the-date card and he or she does not."

Out-of-town guests are the only ones who require a save-the-date card. Feel free to send more, but just be consistent. If you are going to send a card to one groomsman, send them to your entire wedding party. The same goes for work friends and relatives.

The Projects

This save-the-date card was made using a photo of the church and is easily customizable for anyone's wedding. Using PrintingPress Platinum, the digital photograph was inserted as a background image on the front of a 10" x 7" (25.4 x 17.8 cm) folded card. The photo was then converted to black and white for a more dramatic style. The floating text box on the front simply states the date and place of the wedding. Lodging suggestions and travel information are included inside. A pink vellum envelope with a printed address allows the photograph to peek through.

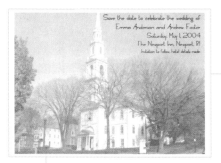

For the bridal shower invitation, a graphic of a wedding dress was enlarged to the full size of the $4\frac{1}{2}$" x $6\frac{1}{4}$" (11.4 x 15.9 cm) invitation. A light pink card and envelope were combined with a slightly darker pink wedding dress graphic and even deeper, darker pink text. The *Beckles Wide* font was used for everything except the bride's name, which is enhanced with the *Sky Pie* font. This invitation can also be made by using a vellum overlay for the text, keeping the wedding dress silhouette on the card stock, and attaching them with a ribbon.

The save-the-date card with the blue border was made by a couple who met while working at an ice cream store. They created an ice cream scoop homage to dish out the wedding "scoop." A checkerboard border matching the color of the scoop handle outlines the $4\frac{1}{2}$" x $6\frac{1}{4}$" (11.4 x 15.9 cm) invitation. The *Jackson Junior Wide* font was used for the entire card. The image of the scoop was added to a white envelope to create a matching set.

Robert and Cynthia Thompson
826 Franklin Street
New York, New York 10002

Photo strips are instantly appealing. They evoke nostalgia, energy, and fun. For this save-the-date card project, a photo strip of the couple was scanned and placed down the left border of the 5" x 7" (12.7 x 17.8 cm) card. The left margin is set for $1\frac{4}{5}$" (4.6 cm), so the text runs as captions to the four photos, telling a story. The font used here is called *Boys on Mopeds* by Jakob Fischer. Its crooked, casual style adds to the playfulness of the photo strip. A rich blue envelope completes a stunning combination.

just the two of us

Stationery for Two

Newlywed stationery is the first chance a married couple has to showcase their freshly joined names. Couples can create formal stationery that coordinates with their wedding invitations to use for thank-you notes, as well as more whimsical, modern, or brightly colored styles to use later for casual correspondence.

   For her wedding invitations, Teresa Araco Rodgers, a philanthropic advisor in Philadelphia, decided she wanted a twist on the traditional. Though her invitations were white, she used blue text and even called her reception a "shindig." "All of our friends loved our invitations and said how 'us' they were. So we decided to make coordinating stationery for our thank-you notes with our new married name," says Teresa. "For me, it was also a way to have my wedding last just a little longer."

Teresa's newlywed stationery uses the same blue text as her wedding invitation. To keep with the modern style of her invitation, the return address is printed on the bottom of the envelope instead of on the envelope flap.

"We used them for our thank-you notes, but I am happy we have plenty left over. We use them to thank friends when we're invited over for dinner or something," says Teresa.

Justine Shembri, a health care executive originally from New Jersey had a different feeling about her newlywed stationery. "We did have 'Fred and Justine' stationery that matched our wedding invitation. I loved it, but we used it all up writing thank-you notes. Shortly after our honeymoon, Fred got a new job, and we moved to Pennsylvania. I felt that we needed different stationery—to reflect not only the new address but the new chapter in our lives."

STATIONERY FOR EVERY SEASON

Many factors contribute to the overall look and feel of your personalized stationery, including the paper color and texture, whether the envelope color matches or coordinates, the font style and color, and the sparing use of a custom-designed monogram. As newlyweds, start with one generic design that you can both use for your thank-you notes.

Don't settle for a single set of stationery to suit every mood and season—be creative over time and design different personal stationery for his or hers, congratulations or condolences, spring or fall. Print extra so you can build up a collection from which to choose when you need to send a note.

TYING THE KNOT AND THE LETTERS

Newlywed stationery is the perfect time to debut a married couple's combined monogram of both first initials and a last initial in the center. (Typically, the bride's initial is first.) Modern etiquette suggests that an engaged couple use this monogram only once they are officially married. Therefore, wedding invitations should only use their individual initials. However, anything made for the wedding reception, such as escort cards, favors, and menu cards, can have their married monogram.

Once the wedding is over, newlywed stationery will come in handy for thank-you notes. In addition to the combined monogram, the couple can use either first names, or just the initial of the groom's last name. The couple can also try out their new Mr. and Mrs. title with their full names, such as "Mr. and Mrs. Sam and

Cynthia Davidson."

DESIGNING YOUR MONOGRAM

The Platinum edition of PrintingPress has a special feature for creating a traditional one-, two-, or three-letter monogram. The tool will format initials using any font, help you customize the size ratio of the outside letters to the middle one, and set how much the letters overlap. See Chapter Seven, "Tools & Techniques," for more information on Platinum's monogram feature.

When designing a monogram, keep in mind the root of the word monogram is mono, which means one. The purpose of a monogram is to take separate initials and create one design. "The idea is not to just stick two or three letters next to each other," says Megan. "You want to create one unified and special design."

As you design your monogram, test several fonts. Often, elegant script fonts are too slanted to use in a monogram. The Platinum monogram tool has a skew feature to adjust the angle of the letters of any font. Alternatively, Mountaincow's unique font, *Erin*, is an upright script font designed specifically for creating monograms.

For a unique or specific monogram, try searching the Internet for downloadable fonts. A wide variety of free fonts, which are available in various degrees of quality, and many beautiful and sophisticated fonts are available for purchase that are not expensive. Consider your budget, and then visit the Design Ideas section of Mountaincow's website for links to font download websites.

Once you've decided on your font, adjust the skew if necessary, then balance the letters by finding the right ratio of the center letter to the outside letters. You can create an attractive, modern look by shrinking the outside letters to be as small as 20 percent of the size of the center letter. Another modern idea is to use all lowercase letters in your monogram. You can also adjust how the outside letters are centered vertically relative to the center letter to create different effects. Even add a border to the monogram for your own twist on a traditional look.

For a more detailed look at personalized stationery, see Chapter Six.

The Projects

All the newlywed stationery envelopes are designed with a return address on the back. In the blue folded note, a small version of the monogram was copied and pasted above the return address.

The monogram on the blue stationery is a clean, formal design using *Copperplate Gothic Light*. The letters are not overlapping—the result of manipulating the "overlap relative to the middle letter" function of the monogram tool in PrintingPress Platinum. The side initials were made 70 percent of the middle letter's size. (See Chapter Seven, "Tools & Techniques," for more information on the monogram tool and how to adjust the size of the monogram.)

EFA
614 HUDSON STREET
NEW YORK, NY 10029

EFA

A flourish script font is used on the green card to spell out "Emma & Andrew." On the pink card, fonts with long tails and swirls create a traditional, elegant monogram.

For a more unisex design, the modern and clean *Beckles Wide* was used on a tall card with the couple's name written vertically down the left margin. Using PrintingPress Platinum, this design was made using a text box with one letter on each line. The card is 4" x 9 1/2" inches (10.1 x 23.5 cm), so it's able to fit in a striking deep-red Number 10 envelope. This size is perfect for mailing with checks or attaching to letter-sized papers.

Modern

Decorative

Elegant

Classic

Whimsical

We joyfully announce
the birth of our daughter

Emma Claire
March 14, 2003
6 pounds, 8 ounces
20 ½ inches

James & Elisabeth Adams

thank You

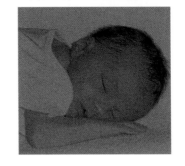
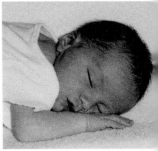
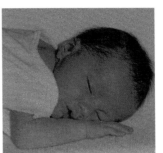

ONCE

UPON

A

TIME

For Baby's First Library

With much love

Laura

Kate Davis
148 Townsend Lane
Anytown, NY 12045

For Baby's First Library

With much love

_____

Samantha's friends
got together and
started a library
for her baby.

Please bring your
favorite children
to her show
Sun

chapter 2

for the new baby

a new addition

A Star Is Born

Megan has been making invitations and announcements on her computer for years. She even made the invitations for her and her husband Josh's engagement party—twelve years ago! When it came time to create a birth announcement for her second child, Jackson, she knew exactly what she wanted.

"I wanted a black-and-white photo with the edges faded into the card, a tiny little ribbon, and simple, elegant text," she says. "But we had just moved, and I had no idea where to buy stationery. I looked online but there was always something wrong—the fonts were too ornate, the photo couldn't be black and white, or it was impossible to add a ribbon."

Instead of giving in, Megan decided once again to make them herself. "We used many different software applications to print the cards, address the envelopes, and create a guide to indicate where to punch holes for the ribbon," she recalls. "Afterwards, we had a million lists around the house, trying to keep track of who gave us what gifts and whether I had sent them a thank-you note yet. Josh and I kept saying that this did not need to be so hard."

The result? Let's just say Mountaincow was born very shortly after Jackson.

WHEN IT COMES TO THE BABY

Megan's quest is common when it comes to making baby announcements. New mom Johanna Skier says, "You think: Price is no object. My baby deserves the best. You don't want to compromise."

So, where to start? The better question might be when to start. "If you're planning to make announcements yourself, be sure to buy everything you can before the baby comes," advises Megan. Johanna agrees, "You can even pre-address and pre-stamp the envelopes."

There is only so much advance preparation you can do, however. "I packed catalogs in my suitcase to bring to the hospital. I was not inclined to pick out announcements before I saw what my baby looked like! Isn't that funny?" says Sue Burdick, a television producer from Chicago. "It's like I had to get a feeling for my baby before I chose something!"

PICTURE THIS

"Birth announcements without a picture are a big fat rip off!" exclaims Stephanie Field, a New Jersey mom who included photos with both her children's birth announcements. "When my friend who lives across the country had a baby, I wanted to see her kid!" she remarks emphatically. "I don't have time to deal with the photos that are emailed to me. I want a picture of your kid in my mailbox. Period."

Many moms agree. Whether they use a digital photo that's been uploaded into a homemade announcement or have the film developer duplicate one a hundred times, they often include a photo of the newborn in the announcement.

One creative mom, Kim Hammer, included a maternity picture of her and an early photo of her baby with a caption that read, before and after. "Many people have told us they still have the announcement on their refrigerator, and Max is one year old!" says Kim.

Wendy Zalinsky, a magazine executive in Connecticut, decided against having pictures of her boys in their announcements. "Newborns aren't that cute," she says. This is why some parents wait a few weeks before taking a photo for the announcement.

NO MUG SHOT

Instead of a photo, Wendy chose a seasonal theme for her most recent announcement. "Charlie was born near Halloween, so I found an announcement with a cute drawing of two boys in a wagon in a pumpkin patch," she says.

Classic birth announcements with just the name, date of birth, weight, and length are always a wonderful and appropriate option. If you're looking for a bit of flair, consider what Johanna was thinking. "My friends know me for adoring Hello Kitty. So when Annie arrived, I created a simple announcement that reads Hello Annie, with all of her info, and a small image of Hello Kitty's face."

BIG BROTHERS AND SISTERS

For a baby who is not your firstborn, you can use the baby's older siblings to introduce the new family member. "Older brothers and sisters should always be included on the announcement because it makes them feel important," says Megan.

"You can list their names alongside yours at the bottom of the announcement."

WHO GETS ONE?

Generally speaking, a birth announcement is sent to all your close friends and family. "We sent Max's birth announcement to the same people on our wedding invitation list. I did get pregnant on our honeymoon, after all!" says Kim. "And, of course, we sent one to our obstetrician. He still has it hanging in his office."

The purpose of sending your announcements is to share your joy, not to solicit baby gifts. "We were careful not to send an announcement to anyone who we thought would feel obligated to send a gift," says Johanna. "We kept it limited to really close friends and family."

THANK-YOU NOTES TO MATCH

No matter how few announcements are sent, new parents are often showered with gifts from well-wishing friends and relatives. While you are planning your announcements, think ahead and create coordinating thank-you notes. Use the same color, design scheme, or font for a simple thank-you card.

"It may be tempting to send a thank-you note with a birth announcement to the friends who gave you gifts right away when the baby was born," says Megan. "But the announcement really deserves to be sent in its own envelope."

PRESENT PERFECT?

Although many new moms find choosing birth announcements to be a very personal choice, handmade birth announcements can make a terrific gift. Custom announcements can be expensive, and having a newborn doesn't allow much time for sleep, let alone printing projects. "My cousin made my announcements for me, and it was a huge, huge help," says Stephanie. "She designed them and involved me, and then she had them printed."

If you're considering making announcements for a friend, ask her if she's already made arrangements, and if not, let her know your intentions. This way she can have input while appreciating your generosity. If she has already taken care of her announcements, offer to make thank-you notes and envelopes. "A friend made us homemade thank-you notes that were really cool and very helpful," says Kim. For mother of two Kim Broggi, the best kind of thank-you notes come pre-addressed and stamped. "If you have access to the guest list of a baby shower, giving pre-addressed thank-you notes is the perfect gift," she says. "Every new mom should hint for it!"

The Project

By taking a traditional baby picture and adding a modern twist, this project recolors and repeats the photo for a Warhol-style treatment. The folding card is 5" x $9\frac{1}{2}$" (12.7 x 24.8 cm) with a vertical fold. The baby's photo was imported once and cropped to about a 1" (2.5 cm) square to correspond to the shape of the card. The image was then copied and pasted three times, with one space separating each image. One at a time, the image was recolored—red, green, blue, and purple.

For the inside of the card, a square block of text was created by justifying the floating text box both horizontally and vertically. Using *Beckles Wide* font, all the text was created in 18-point font, with two lines left blank for the baby's name. In a separate text box, the baby's name was created in 34-point font and justified to match the rest of the text.

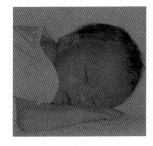
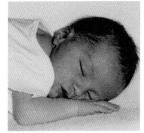
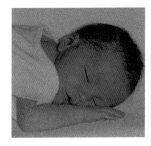
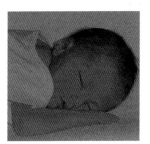

We joyfully announce
the birth of our daughter

Emma Claire

March 14, 2003
6 pounds, 8 ounces
20 ½ inches

James & Elisabeth Adams

Robert and Cynthia Thompson
826 Franklin Street
New York, New York 10002

The font used for the envelope is the same as that used on the announcement. Keeping design elements consistent across multiple pieces of an invitation results in a coordinated and professional look.

The thank-you note is created in a similar manner, but it has a horizontal fold to distinguish it from the birth announcement. The text below the four photos used *Beckles Wide* font and was justified to create the same look as the announcement.

once upon a time

B is for ... Books

When New York native Andrea Crane's best friend Mimi was expecting, she wanted to throw a shower that would not only prepare Mimi for the baby's arrival but would also be fun for everyone at the party. She headed straight to a craft store and picked up an assortment of fabric paints, then asked the guests to bring packages of plain white onesies in various sizes. In addition to the great gifts her guests brought, Mimi went home with more than a dozen onesies hand designed by her closest friends. Her favorite one reads: You think I'm cute, you should see my Aunt Jenny.

Jen DeGraphenreed, a second-generation English teacher, has always had a love of books. It was no surprise, then, that when her sister-in-law and niece threw her a baby shower, they asked all the guests to bring a book to start the little one's library.

"I remember going to the children's library with my mother and being overwhelmed by the endless selection that I could take home with me. They were like little treasures," remembers Jen. "My favorite part of my shower was revisiting books from my own childhood that I had forgotten."

JUDGE AN INVITATION BY ITS COVER

If you are asking every guest to bring something unique and essential to the theme of your party, it's important to include clear instructions in the invitation. Also, if your guests are going to be painting, let them know so they can dress appropriately.

For a book-themed party, make the invitation look like a book. Find a font in which all the capital letters are ornate, like those used in old-fashioned storybooks. This font will also serve as the decorative item on the invitation.

THEMES AND ACTIVITIES OPTIONAL

For some, a shower without a theme is like a baby without a diaper. Others feel differently. "I was thankful just to keep my feet up and be served with food and presents," says Kim Hammer. "I was really thankful not to have to play games. Themes should be limited to color or decorating schemes, not games or activities."

Kim Broggi, a teacher from New Jersey, believes there can be an appropriate time or place for themed showers. "I went to a shower for someone from work where the gifts related to a time of day—bathtime, bedtime, feeding time. It turned out really well because as work friends, we needed a little more help with what to get her."

THE REGISTRY ISSUE

The million-dollar question: Should you include on the invitation where the new parents are registered? According to standard etiquette, registry information should never be printed.

"I definitely think moms-to-be should register; otherwise, you'll get nothing but clothes," says Kim Hammer. "But I don't think it should be printed on the invitation. That's kind of tacky. It's better to just have the host inform people by word of mouth."

Of course, modern-day pragmatists have come up with a compromise. "You can include registry information on a separate card and enclose it with the invitation," suggests Megan. "Realistically, do we want to answer a million phone calls with the same question? No one has time for that these days."

FOR BABY'S FIRST LIBRARY

WITH MUCH LOVE

Laura

KATE DAVIS
148 TOWNSEND LANE
ANYTOWN, NNY 12345

ONCE
UPON
A
TIME

FOR BABY'S FIRST LIBRARY

WITH MUCH LOVE

_____

FIRST

SAMANTHA'S FRIENDS
GOT TOGETHER AND
STARTED A LIBRARY
FOR HER BABY.

PLEASE BRING YOUR
FAVORITE CHILDREN'S BOOK
TO HER SHOWER ON
SUNDAY, SEPTEMBER 22 AT
2:00 P.M.
148 TOWNSEND LANE

REGRETS ONLY:
KATE DAVIS 555-1212

For another type of storybook shower, turn to Mother Goose. The age old rhymes are always a good place to start for a shower theme and can provide sweet ideas for decorations, games and what to serve. With an image of a dish running away with the spoon, this $4\frac{1}{2}$" x $6\frac{1}{4}$" (11.4 x 15.9 cm) invitation uses a rhyme for the party details. The white card is paired with a dusty blue A6 envelope. The image is repeated on the $3\frac{1}{2}$" x 5" (8.9 x 12.7 cm) registry card. Coordinating thank you notes make a fantastic gift for the expecting guest of honor. Use the same dish and spoon image on folded $8\frac{1}{2}$" x $5\frac{1}{2}$" (21.6 x 14 cm) cards and print the addresses of the guest list on dusty blue A2 envelopes. Wrap them with a ribbon and tuck in a few books of stamps.

Registry card

Jane & Peter
are registered at Babies 'R' Us
under the name Stevens

Folded thank-you note

thank you

Hey diddle diddle, hearing their baby's giggle
will send Jane & Peter's hearts over the moon.

We hope you'll join us for brunch
to see all the fun that's happened
since the dish ran away with the spoon.

Sunday, September 18, 11:00 a.m.
125 Main Street

RSVP to Susan Adams 555-1234

Invitation

Robert and Cynthia Thompson
826 Franklin Street
New York, New York 10002

Envelope

The Project

The book-style baby shower invitation is an 8½" x 5½" (21.6 x 14 cm) folded card printed on both sides. Two were printed on an 8½" x 11" (21.6 x 27.9 cm) piece of card stock and then cut it in half. The outside of the invitation used a decorative font called *Flower Garden* by Bree Gorton. This created an ornate O for "Once upon a time," and for the text inside. The blue envelope matches the blue ink on the invitation.

The best part about this invitation is that each set includes a book label for the guest to write her name on and glue inside the book she brings to the shower. The book tag is 3" x 3" (7.6 x 7.6 cm) and uses the same paper, font, and ink color as the invitation.

Invitation (outside)

ONCE
UPON
A
TIME

Invitation (inside)

SAMANTHA'S FRIENDS GOT TOGETHER AND STARTED A LIBRARY FOR HER BABY.

PLEASE BRING YOUR FAVORITE CHILDREN'S BOOK TO HER SHOWER ON SUNDAY, SEPTEMBER 22 AT 2:00 P.M.
148 TOWNSEND LANE

REGRETS ONLY:
KATE DAVIS 555-1212

Book Label

FOR BABY'S FIRST LIBRARY

WITH MUCH LOVE

_____

Envelope

CYNTHIA THOMPSON
826 FRANKLIN STREET
NEW YORK, NEW YORK 10002

Sugar and spice and everything nice,
That's what our Sofia is made of!

Please help us wish our sweet-ie-pie
a happy third birthday.

Sunday, August 8
4:00 p.m.
68 State Street

rsvp: 752-555-2999

Alexis

thank you!

It's time to party!

Alexis

wants you to join her at her

sweet 16

Meet her at Wurlitzer's

Saturday May 15, 2004

We invite you to join us
when our son

Joshua Evan

is called to the Torah
as a Bar Mitzvah

Saturday, September 15
Nine o'clock
The Temple Beth Israel
Six Markus Lane
Chatham, NJ

Fred and Joyce Graybell

please reply by September 1

Robert and Cynthia
Thompson

Robert and
New Yor

820

The Graybells
612 Morris Avenue
Chatham, NJ 04958

MAZEL TO

chapter 3

for the birthday girl or boy

guess who's one?

The First Birthday

For Leah Mack, turning one year old meant much more than just birthday cake and presents. Her parents had a candle-lighting service, a baby naming, and a wish ceremony.

"The truth is, this was the first time all of her grandparents were in the same place since she was born, and it was the first chance to really celebrate the joining of our families and the connections throughout the generations," explains Leah's mom Stephanie Field. "This was also my chance to talk about the meaning of her name and who she is named after."

For the wish ceremony, Stephanie asked all her relatives to write down a wish for Leah on a slip of paper and then collected them in a silver baby cup. Leah just celebrated her third birthday, and those wishes haven't moved. "I haven't decided what I want to do with them yet, but I'd like to present them to her at some milestone event," Stephanie says.

Whether you include the standard traditions or create your own, a baby's first birthday is a monumental day that can be shared in a number of ways. Some parents keep the celebration small and include only close relatives. Other parents throw a large party and invite all their friends and family.

SIZE MATTERS

Jennifer Laduca, a clinical psychologist and mother of Caitlin, went back and forth on what size to make Caitlin's first birthday party. "There are so many things about the first year of a baby's life that makes you worry that we wanted to celebrate Caitlin (and us!) literally surviving to age one," Jennifer says. "It was a milestone for all of us."

For some families, a smaller party makes more sense. "We had the large, fancy christening, so we had a small, intimate birthday," says Maureen Petrellese, a mortgage broker and mother of two.

Smaller parties often go without invitations to keep the vibe low-key. "We didn't send invitations because it might have been viewed as a formal affair, and the extended family would have been hurt that they didn't receive one," says Maureen. "And for smaller gatherings I tend to do everything at the last minute, so I just call the guests."

Even if you forgo the invites, using your computer can help with other last-minute details, such as thank-you notes. "Take photos of your child ripping open her gifts—this makes a perfect shot to use on a thank-you note," suggests Megan. "Of course, if you do print invitations, make sure to print extras to send to out-of-town relatives who appreciate the thought of being included, even though they can't come."

WHY D.I.Y.?

Kate Wallace, a Philadelphia mom, has straddled both camps for first birthdays. For her son Will, she invited only immediate family to celebrate his first year. By the time her daughter Sophie turned one, her social circle had grown and it made more sense to invite everyone. But despite the size difference of the parties, she made the invitations for both.

"I think it's fun to make your own. You get so many fill-in-the-blank invitations these days," Kate says. For Sophie, she had a different reason. "It was probably my last opportunity to have a say in what the invitations look like. By the time they are two, they have their own opinions!"

Alexis is turning one!

Please join us for cupcakes to celebrate!

Saturday, July 13
3:00 p.m.
826 Franklin Street

RSVP 555.1212
Robert and Cynthia Thompson

Thank you from Alexis

PARTY TIME

Whatever your celebration entails, be sure it doesn't take place during your child's naptime. "Caitlin's nap was all messed up the day of her party so she was cranky and miserable," says Jennifer. "It made me feel guilty for throwing the party."

Remember that the first birthday party is still more about relatives than the birthday boy or girl. The food can cater to adult tastes as long as you have a few tidbits for the little ones as well.

Also, don't worry if the most convenient date is on a weekend surrounding the birthday. "Having the party on a weekend makes sense for your guests and gives you and your spouse the opportunity to have a cake without the crowd on your child's actual birthday," notes Megan. "Our kids each got to eat their first cupcake on their first birthday, which can be a hilarious and messy event you get to share with them privately."

The Project

A cupcake with a single candle is the simple yet perfect image for this first birthday party invitation. The sweet *Sky Pie* font is used for the text on the invitation, the thank-you note, and the envelope.

Invitation card

The invitation is 4½" x 5½" (10.8 x 14 cm), printed four at a time on pink letter-size paper. The thank-you note, 5½" x 8½"(14 x 21.6 cm), folds to the same size as the invitation and can use the same A2 envelope as the invitation.

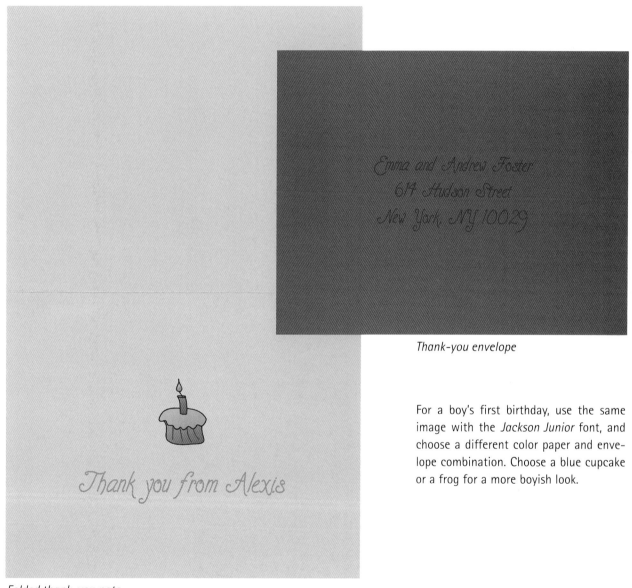

Thank-you envelope

Folded thank-you note

For a boy's first birthday, use the same image with the *Jackson Junior* font, and choose a different color paper and envelope combination. Choose a blue cupcake or a frog for a more boyish look.

Gramma's brag book of:
...fia's third birthday
August 5, 2004

Sugar and spice and everything nice,
That's what our Sofia is made of!

Please help us wish our sweetie-pie
a happy third birthday.

Sunday, August 5
4:00 p.m.
58 State Street

rsvp: 732-555-2999

Alexis

Alexis

thank you!

sweets for the sweetie

Celebrating Another Year

Throwing birthday parties for your kids every year is a lot of work. Expectations run high, and you want the parents to have as much fun as the kids so they'll come back again the next year. Start the planning with professional-looking invitations that you make on your computer to introduce the theme, ignite the excitement, and, best of all, save time and money.

For many parents, throwing birthday parties is a two- or three-times-a-year requirement. "If you're still using fill-in invites, that's a lot of 'who, what, where, and whens' to fill in," says Megan. "If I don't have to handwrite anything, I don't even mind sending courtesy invitations to out-of-town relatives who I know won't be able to attend."

A REVOLUTIONARY CHANGE

Gone are the days when your hands cramp from filling in the same party information over and over—before you even start addressing the envelopes.

"Every year I swear I am going to be economical," says Lauren Barnett, a Florida mom on the third-birthday-party circuit, thanks to her daughter Zoe. "I swear I am going to keep party costs down so I pick out the fill-in cards. Then I remember how much work they are."

Avoiding the manual labor of handwriting invitations without paying for custom printing is just one benefit to using a computer to print your invitations. If you use PrintingPress, the address book and mailing list features guarantee you'll never handwrite another envelope again. See Chapter Seven, "Tools & Techniques," for more information about PrintingPress's address book and mailing list.

GETTING STARTED

Right now, Lauren is in full-swing planning for Zoe's birthday party. This year, Zoe's theme is arts and crafts. "The first thing you have to do is figure out where you're having the party. If you're thinking of having it at a restaurant or children's gym, you have to schedule that in advance."

The theme you choose greatly affects the paper and graphics you need for the invitations. By coordinating the invitations, activities, food, and favors under a common theme, you can turn a simple party into a memorable event.

FINDING A DATE

Planning should begin about six weeks before the party, and invitations should be sent out three weeks in advance. You will need a week or two to select and buy paper, find graphics, and experiment with the invitations. Leave at least one afternoon to actually do the printing once everything else is ready.

According to Linda Kaye, creator of www.partymakers.com, plan the party as close to your child's real birthday as possible. Be sure to check with your child's school calendar and vacations so there are no conflicts, and ensure the friends most special to your child will be able to attend.

The time of day to have your party is also an important decision. "If you don't want to serve a meal," suggests Linda, "have the party in the morning to end by 11:30 a.m. or begin around 1:30 p.m." For younger children, plan for a 90-minute party; older kids can last a few hours.

THE GUEST LIST

If you're unsure of who to invite and don't want to hurt anyone's feelings, invite your child's entire class. This way, your child can pass out the invitations in school. See Chapter Seven, "Tools & Techniques," to learn how to use PrintingPress to address envelopes with just names and no street address.

If you were planning for a smaller gathering, you can limit the party to just boys or girls. If you are having a co-ed event, avoid using an overly "girly" invitation. "We didn't think the boys would be upset about missing Sabrina's princess party," says Megan. These invitations should be fully addressed and sent through the mail.

The Invitation

Next comes the fun part: You have your date and place—now it's time for a theme. "Kids will usually choose a television character or fairy tale," says Lauren. Surf the web for simple color photos or graphics, and copy and paste them into your computer invitation projects. You can do this by right-clicking your mouse on the graphic and selecting Copy in the pop-up menu that appears. Then open your project and paste the image onto the invitation. Be sure to check the copyright information before using images for professional or business purposes.

The Internet is also a great tool if your child is too young to choose or you feel stumped for ideas. "There are many websites out there with lists and lists of fun ideas for party themes," says Megan. "They often have fun food and game ideas to carry it out."

Megan recommends choosing a graphic that can be used on every element of the party. In the sample project shown, the lollypop image adorned the invitation, the thank-you note, place cards, and goody bag tag. "The repetition of the graphic will help pull everything together," says Megan. This idea can grow with your child. As their favorite characters change, so can the graphics.

Next, prepare what you need to include on the invitation. Take advantage of being in charge: Present your information in rhyme, as a song, or full of references to your theme.

In addition to the time and place of the party, have clear drop-off and pick-up times for the parents, suggests Linda. Also have very descriptive directions included to avoid any latecomers. If you live far from your guests, you might want to create little maps from a direction service website to include in the invitation.

Also be sure to include a phone number or email address as well as the RSVP date. The more accurately you predict the number of guests to expect, the less stress you will have about having too much or too little food or favors. (Linda suggests having five extra favors on hand, just in case.)

SMOOTH SAILING

"I went nuts last year," admits Lauren. "This year I just want to relax and take pictures." Snap-happy moms and dads should prepare their cameras in advance to make sure they have enough film and batteries. Lauren plans to enlist the help of other grown-ups this year so she doesn't stress during the party. Ask other parents, aunts and uncles, or even babysitters to join the party to have extra hands.

"You'll want to enjoy the party," advises Lauren. "Some moms spend so much money and are stressed and miserable the whole time. There's a chance your child will play off your emotions—or they're too young to know what's going on anyway. So just have fun with it."

For a younger child, Lauren suggests sharing the celebration with another birthday boy or girl. "Throwing a party with another child can make things easier. There will be plenty of adults to help, and believe me, neither child will be short of attention!"

Linda recommends making nametags for all your little guests. "You and the entertainers will have much better luck keeping the partygoers' attention if you can call them by name," says Linda. "It will also be easier for them to get to know one another if you are combining friends from a variety of locales."

Linda also suggests setting the table before guests arrive and preparing as much of the food in advance as you can. You can even keep scooped ice cream in the freezer, or pour the juice and store it on a tray out of the way.

Invitation

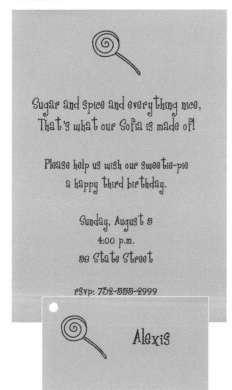

Goody bag tag

The Project

With your theme in mind, buy printer-compatible stationery or find appropriate card stock for the invitation. The featured project uses a two-toned paper that is lime green on one side and hot pink on the other, creating a color scheme for the party. The invitation was designed on the lime green side of the paper in hot pink ink to match the other side of the card stock. The font, *Girls are Weird* by John Martz, and the lollypop graphic were used on all the stationery to complete the theme.

Because the invitation was cut from an $8\frac{1}{2}$" x 11" (21.6 x 27.9 cm) sheet down to 5" x 7" (12.7 x 17.8 cm), the leftover pieces were used for paper cup assignments and goody bag tags. Once the invitations have been sent and the RSVPs are tallied, create the paper cup assignments and goody bag tags as if you were making place cards. See Chapter Seven, "Tools & Techniques," to learn more about making place cards using PrintingPress.

To assign the children's seats (and to make sure the children drink their own juice), create a place card measuring $8\frac{1}{2}$" x 2" (21.6 x 5.1 cm) so it wraps around a paper cup.

Thank-you note

For the goody bag tags, make place cards measuring 4" x $2\frac{1}{2}$" (25.4 x 6.4 cm). Print out the children's names on the individual cards, and punch a hole in the corner of each card through which you can thread a ribbon to attach it to the goody bag.

After the party, create a thank-you note to coordinate with your invitation and theme. Using the same card stock or a coordinating paper, create a folded note card with the birthday boy or girl's name on it.

Finally, to thank the other grown-ups you recruited to help with the party, make them a "brag book" of the photos you took at the party. Make the cover using the program template, which measures $6\frac{1}{2}$" x 9" (15.9 x 22.9 cm). Make both the fold orientation and the ribbon hole orientation horizontal. To create the inside pages, make blank pages slightly smaller than the cover—6" x $8\frac{1}{2}$" (15.2 x 21.6 cm). You can import digital photos or scanned prints into PrintingPress and print them right on the pages. Another approach is to glue the photographs or use photo corners to attach them to blank pages. Punch holes at the markers and string the pages together with a ribbon.

Paper cup tag

a milestone event

A Rite to Celebrate

Almost every culture or religion has a ceremony to celebrate a child's passage into adulthood. Latin women mark their fifteenth birthday with a ceremonial *Quinceañera*. Native Americans enjoy a four-day ritual of singing, dancing, and praying. A Hindu girl's maternal grandmother hosts a ceremony to present her with her first full-length sari. Holy communion in the Catholic Church welcomes a youth as an active member of the congregation, and a Confirmation ceremony further celebrates his or her faith. Jewish boys and girls celebrate their thirteenth birthday by singing their first public Torah reading at their Bar or Bat Mitzvah, the culmination of years of Hebrew study and months of practice. For many families, these events present an occasion to throw a massive party in celebration.

PRIDE AND JOY

"When you have an occasion such as a Bar Mitzvah, the invitation should come from the heart," says Sherry Schweitzer, owner of A Touch of Class, an event-planning company on Long Island, New York. "It's a day of great pride for the parents, and they should express that in the wording of the invitation."

Sherry also thinks it's appropriate to have the invitation come from the Bar or Bat Mitzvah child. "This day is all about the child. Why not have him or her write the invitation in the first person? Have the reply envelopes in his or her name, too," says Sherry. "The more you get the child involved, the better. After all, it's all for him or her."

Once you've decided on the wording, customize the invitation to reflect the child's personality and interests. "One of Mountaincow's customer's sons is really

interested in architecture," says Megan. "So for his Bar Mitzvah invitation, she scanned a blueprint to use as a background image and then found a perfect drafting font to use." To carry out the theme at the party, she made each table the name of a famous architect, such as Frank Lloyd Wright and Le Corbusier, instead of using numbers.

THE KIDS' PARTY

"It's popular to have a separate party for all the kids the day after the actual Bar Mitzvah," says Sherry. "This way you can cater to the different music and food tastes of the younger crowd and probably save money at the same time."

By using your computer to make your invitations, you can customize what you send. You can make one version of the invitation for the adults and then change the information for the kids if they are having a separate party.

PrintingPress allows you to duplicate a piece of stationery or an entire project so can have as many versions as you want. To duplicate stationery, choose *Duplicate Stationery* from the *Stationery* menu and rename the copy. To duplicate an entire project, choose *Duplicate Project* from the *File* menu.

Alternatively, you could use a single project and create a master invitation card for the Bar Mitzvah, as well as a smaller 4" x 6" (10.2 x 15.2 cm) card with the details of the adult party and a different one with the details of the kids' party to stuff in the appropriate envelopes.

FINDING RELIGION

You may wish to add graphics of religious symbols to the invitations. A great way to find a large selection of graphics is to use your Internet search engine's Images option and type the name of the symbol for the search, such as Star of David. You

please reply by September 1

We invite you to join us
when our son
Joshua Evan
is called to the Torah
as a Bar Mitzvah

Saturday, September 15
Nine o'clock
The Temple Beth Israel
Six Markus Lane
Chatham, NJ

Fred and Joyce Graybell

Robert and Cynthia
Thompson

The Graybells
612 Morris Avenue
Chatham, NJ 04958

Robert an
820
New York

MAZEL TOV

will be amazed at the quantity and quality of graphics from which you can choose.

You can also use your digital camera to take a photo of the church or synagogue to use on your invitation. Use PrintingPress Platinum to add the photo as a background image, and then type over it in an area of foliage around the building. If the photo is dark, you can recolor the text to white so you can see it over the photo.

You can also use a Hebrew font to enhance the invitation with the child's Hebrew name or with a quote or prayer. Visit www.mountaincow.com for details on Mountaincow's selection of original Hebrew fonts.

DO ME A FAVOR

Often the friends of the honoree are given a favor to bring home. "I recommend useful favors," Sherry says. "Kids actually use mouse pads, mirrors, and picture frames. I like to give them choices."

Use PrintingPress's place card feature to put each friend's name on a favor. For instance, if giving out picture frames, make a place card the size of the picture and place it inside the frame. The frame can also double as a table seating plaque for the party.

The Project

The invitation is a 5" x 7" (12.7 x 17.8 cm) card with a Star of David graphic. The body of text is fully justified on both sides—a feature available in PrintingPress Platinum. All the text except for the Bar Mitzvah boy's name has been typed into the text box in 18-point font. Two lines have been skipped where the boy's name will be inserted in a separate text box in a 35-point font. When the name is positioned in the appropriate space, both text boxes can be selected to perfectly align them to the center of the stationery and to each other. Choose *Select all floating images* in the *Edit* menu, and then choose *Align Horizontally Center* in the *Design* menu.

We invite you to join us
when our son

Joshua Evan

is called to the Torah
as a Bar Mitzvah

Saturday, September 15
Nine o'clock
The Temple Beth Israel
Six Markus Lane
Chatham, NJ

Fred and Joyce Graybell

Invitation card

The Star of David is also used on the response card, in the bottom-right corner of the 3½" x 5" (8.9 x 12.7 cm) card. The same font and text color are used on the response card, table place card, and invitation. The color of the envelopes for the response card and the invitation match not only each other but also the ink used on the invitation.

Robert and Cynthia
Thompson

Place card

please reply by September 1

The Graybells
612 Morris Avenue
Chatham, NJ 04958

Response envelope

Response card

...and never been kissed

Roll out the Red Carpet

Is anyone surprised that a popular theme for sweet sixteen parties is, well, drama? According to Risa Meyer and Melinda Konopko, owners of PlumParty.com, an online store of entertaining essentials, their Hollywood party kit that originated for academy-award-viewing parties is a huge hit with the teen set. "It's used for graduation parties and sweet sixteens," says Melinda, "Basically, anywhere 'You're the star' fits." Melinda credits their sales growth to today's fascination with celebrities' lives. "We had a girl who was really interested in filmmaking, so our clapboard key rings really worked for her," says Risa.

Keeping the theme about the host and within an element that the guests can relate to is paramount, according to Risa. "We aim to make parties an extension of the person they are celebrating. We try to find something unique about the sweet sixteen and expand on it. This way, she feels original and special."

IT'S NOT EASY BEING GREEN

Aside from a driver's license, how is a sixteenth birthday party different from any other? "This is the first time girls are really in charge of planning a party," says Risa. "They are really excited about their sweet sixteen, and they're involved in the process in a way they never had been before." So this is the perfect chance to let your teen test her skills as an invitation designer. Once you've settled on a budget and a date, make sure to let her make her share of the decisions. After she's chosen her theme, go to a stationery or paper supply store and see what suits her mood and style. Give her freedom to think creatively and select unusual combinations.

One place your daughter may need help—but not want it—is in drawing up the guest list. When she was younger, you probably made her invite everyone in her class to birthday parties; you don't want to hurt anyone's feelings. Now that she's older, she's the one telling you who to invite, so you may want to remind her that excluding classmates from the guest list will still hurt feelings. No party—no matter how fun—is worth losing friends over.

The invitations should be created and mailed three weeks before the event. Use the invitations to hint at what guests should expect and to build excitement about the party. You can make the party as casual or as formal as you like. If you decide to have a more adult party with a meal, let your daughter create fun table identification cards or even place cards for the guests.

Party favors are always guest favorites at big events, so encourage your daughter to get creative and make personalized gifts to give as favors. She can repeat the party colors and create personalized stationery for each of her friends. For gift tags, create a place card with a text box so that the card reads, "<guest name> had a blast at Alexis's sweet 16."

It's time to party!
Alexis
wants you to join her at her
sweet 16
Meet her at Wurlitzer's
Saturday May 15, 2004
on Rt 27 in Somerset
seven o'clock
until the party's over
R.S.V.P. alexis@alexis.com

Alexis Thompson
826 Franklin Street
New York, NY 10013

Every good hostess, no matter her age, sends thank you notes for gifts. Coordinating a thank you note with the party's invitation is always in good taste, but it's just as appropriate to create stationery that fits the personality of the person writing the note. In this case, the teenager celebrating her Sweet Sixteen opted for a pair of flirty lips to seal her notes with a kiss. Her name is written with the *SkyPie* font in a bright orange. Her pink and orange color palate repeats on the back of the envelope where her return address is topped with a small pair of lips.

Thank-you envelope

Thank-you note

The Project

The generous margins, justified text, and varying point sizes make an otherwise simple invitation look exciting and full of energy. The $4\frac{1}{2}$" x $6\frac{1}{4}$" (11.4 x 15.9 cm) flat card has a $\frac{3}{4}$" (1.9 cm) margin on the right and left and a $1\frac{1}{4}$" (3.2 cm) margin on the top and bottom. With these margins as strict guides, manipulate the text boxes to create one solid box of text. Five text boxes are used for the varying point sizes, all using *Jackson Junior Sans Wide*. Use a font size around 16 points for all the general information, and then create separate text boxes for the information you want to stand out. In this example, "Alexis" is 71 points and "sweet 16" is 44.

The dark purple text on the lavender card ties in the coordinating envelope. Once the invitation is printed, a corner punch purchased at an office supply store rounds the corners for a softer style.

Emma and Andrew Foster
614 Hudson Street
New York, NY 10029

Envelope

It's time to party!
Alexis
wants you to join her at her
sweet 16
Meet her at Wurlitzer's
Saturday May 15, 2004
on Rt 27 in Somerset
seven o'clock
until the party's over
R.S.V.P. alexis@alexis.com

Invitation

the big zero

Monumental Birthdays

"My fiancée treats her birthday like a national holiday. In fact, she treats everyone's birthday like that. So when she was turning 30, I knew I had my work cut out for me," says Chris Brahe, a sales executive in New York.

"The first thing I did was enlist her mom, and she was an invaluable source. She had some priceless childhood photos. I had a hard time choosing which one to use on the invitation."

Using a childhood photo for an adult's party invitation adds humor and sentiment to the event. It can be fun to revisit childhood memories as well as favorite characters, books, and foods.

In the end, Chris decided to go for a shot of his fiancée at about 6 years old, sleeping with a Snoopy doll tucked under one arm. "The scary thing is," Chris admits, "she still loves Snoopy, so I knew all her friends would get a kick out of that photo. For the party, we bought Snoopy napkins to tie it together."

CONVERSATION STARTERS

Another idea, as shown in the sample project, is to give guests a chance to think up their favorite stories of the birthday boy or girl in advance. Provide a card with the invitation for guests to write down their tales and easily have them handy when it is time for the toasts—or the roast.

Because parties often mix groups of people who have never met—such as family, friends, and coworkers—nametags can be extremely handy. They can also help spread the theme of the party if you include the same image that was used on the invitation.

YOU'RE NEVER TOO OLD FOR A THEME.

To throw a party to remember, consider a unique theme personal to the guest of honor. This will also give you a springboard for thinking up creative drinks and decorations that will make the party stand out.

For example, if your guest of honor loves to surf, re-create an island mystique using Mai Tais with umbrellas, hibiscus centerpieces, candles on bamboo stakes and some authentic Hawaiian specialty foods. If he's a gambler and a trip to Vegas is out of the question, go for a hip night club scene complete with cheesy lounge singer and a for-charity black jack or craps table.

Of course, the best way to introduce a theme is to start with the invitation. Use hibiscus graphics or photos on the Hawaii invitations and invite everyone on a virtual trip to the Islands. Include a pair of playing cards in the Vegas invitation and ask everyone to vote on their favorite charity as recipient of proceeds from the event. You can even recommend donations rather than bringing presents. But beware, once you throw one excellent bash, expectations (and attendance) will be even higher for your next party.

Robert and Cynth[...]
826 Franklin[...]
New York, NY[...]

muchas gracias

...his one time...

Robert
Frank's friend from work

Please join us to celebrate
Frank's 40th Fiesta!
Saturday May 22, 7:30pm
[Ca]sa Mexicana, 7 Livingston Street
[Bri]ng your favorite Frank story
on the enclosed card

[RSVP] to Anna 555-8691

The Project

For Frank's fortieth fiesta, the theme was created by the venue. Held at a Mexican restaurant, margarita and lime images were used on all the party stationery. The invitation was made using an 8½" x 11" (21.6 x 27.9 cm) piece of white card stock, printing four invitations per page and then trimming them down. The simple margarita image was made more festive by a fun, freehand style font called *Jesse Strong* by Mountaincow in the same green as the envelopes.

Please join us to celebrate
Frank's 40th Fiesta!

Saturday May 22, 7:30pm
Rosa Mexicana, 7 Livingston Street

Bring your favorite Frank story
on the enclosed card

R.S.V.P. to Anna 555-8691

Robert and Cynthia Thompson
826 Franklin Street
New York, NY 10012

Invitation

Enclosed with the invitation was a separate card of the same size on which guests could write their favorite story about the guest of honor. The nametags were made by creating a $4\frac{1}{2}$" x 3" (11.3 x 7.6 cm) place card and adding the guests' names from the mailing list. They can then be printed onto individual mailing labels for guests to wear.

Thank-you note

A coordinating thank-you note was designed with an enlarged version of the lime image from the invitation. The same lime green envelopes were used for the invitations and the thank-you notes.

This one time...

Guest story card

Robert
Frank's friend from work

Guest name tag

Cynthia

you bring the confetti,
we'll bring the champagne!

please join us to greet 2004

december 31
8:00 pm
614 hudson street

rsvp 555.5245

joy
bliss
delight
felicity
gladness
happiness
prosperity
love
peace

Hello my pretty!
Don't miss Rob and Nikki's
4th Annual Haunted House+Hay Ride
Saturday October 31
7:30 pm at Brewster's Farm on Easton Avenue
rsvp robnik@ mewflatincow

Hello my

be mine

A mother's love determines how
We love ourselves and others
There is no sky we'll ever see
Not lit by that first love

Turlough O'Carolan

be mine

Please join me for a feast
on a blanket under a shady tree.

This Sunday, 11:00 a.m.

Prepare for a day of pampering
and, of course, brownies.

I love you.

chapter 4

for all seasons

'tis the season

Making Holiday Cheer

"I'm a do-it-yourselfer, plus I like to save a buck!" laughs Lisa Hasbrook, a mother of two who lives outside of Atlanta, Georgia. This past Christmas season she bought cards in which she could slide a photo of her children, but when she was told how much it would cost to print the insides with the special message she wanted, she had a better plan. "I knew I could do it at home and put whatever I wanted inside," said Lisa.

When it comes to her holiday party invitations, Lisa prints the basic inside greeting but prefers to design the outside of the cards herself using rubber stamps. "I used to have the hardest time trying to format the cards and figuring out which part was the inside. I would have to wait for my husband to come home to make me a template," she admits. "I can do it myself now."

Renda Marsh, a flight attendant for Southwest Airlines, will also turn to her computer to help her with the holidays. "Last year I didn't even send out holiday cards," she admits. "But this year I want to do something that will be really personal."

MEET YOUR NEW ASSISTANT

Besides making your holiday cards, your computer can help you dress up a Thanksgiving table, keep track of gifts, and even make gift tags.

"We normally have everyone to our house for the holidays," Renda says. "We don't have a large family, so I thought it would be kind of special to do things differently this year, just for a little change of pace. I am going to make place cards for the seating arrangements. I also want to make tags for the actual dishes. Instead of everything set up how it normally is, I want to have the dishes labeled, such as 'Grandma's sweet potatoes.'"

WISH YOU WERE HERE

For a creative shortcut during the holidays, instead of sending invitations and holiday cards in envelopes, design them as postcards.

"It's perfect for an informal event, such as a Halloween hay ride," says Megan. "It's not appropriate for when you want to reach out and send heartfelt holiday greetings to everyone, but for a quick invite, it's perfect."

To create a postcard in PrintingPress, choose a 4½" x 5½" (10.8 x 14 cm) card and print four per page. Once you've designed your card, print them out on an 8½" x 11" (21.6 x 27.9 cm) sheet of paper and cut them out. On the computer, create a one-sided envelope the same size as the card so that the return address is on the front. Insert your postcards into your printer as if they were envelopes and print.

PIN YOUR HOPES

"Including unusual elements in an invitation or holiday card really makes it stand out," says Megan. "If you're having a tree-trimming party, tie a small sprig of spruce to the card to send the wonderful evergreen scent and get your guests in the holiday mood."

If you're looking for novel ways to embellish the ordinary during the holidays, look no further than your sewing kit. To add a bit of silver to a plain invitation, try inserting a safety pin. Adding grommets or actually sewing your invitations with a needle and thread will grab your guests' attention as well. Make sure you print hole markers to help you add your embellishments in the right place every time.

Cynthia

you bring the confetti,
we'll bring the champagne!

please join us to greet 2004

december 31

8:00 pm

614 hudson street

r.svp 555-3245

joy

bliss

delight

felicity

gladness

happiness

prosperity

love

peace

Joshua, Megan
Sabrina & Jackson

Hello my pretty!
Don't miss Rob and Nikki's
4th Annual Haunted House+Hay Ride

Saturday, October 31
7:30 pm at Brewster's Farm on Easton Avenue
rsvp robnik@mountaincow.com

Projects

This pink holiday card was made to fit in a red number 10 envelope. The words used in the card are arranged to create the shape of a Christmas tree, with a small star graphic placed at the top. The family's names are fully justified at the bottom—a Platinum edition feature—to stand apart from the rest of the card.

Holiday envelope

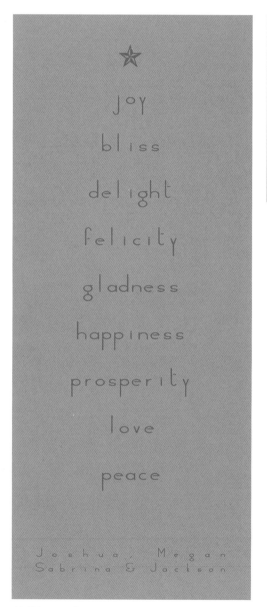

The Halloween party postcard is printed four to a page on orange card stock. The mood of this invitation is created entirely by its spooky font, *A Charming Font* by A. Hölfed. A flying bat was added, sized down to 6 percent of its actual size, and rotated by 18 degrees to the left to have a more swooping element. This bat was copied and pasted to the other side of the card and then flipped horizontally.

Holiday card

Halloween postcard

The New Year's Eve party invitation was created using a 5" x 7" (12.7 x 17.8 cm) sheet of pearlescent vellum attached to a same size piece of pink card stock with a safety pin. The text, in a distinctive font named *Vargas*, is printed directly on the vellum. The top margin is 1" (2.5 cm). Ribbon hole markers, $\frac{1}{8}$" (.3 cm) circles used as guides for the safety pin, were made $\frac{1}{2}$" (1.9 cm) from the top of the card, $\frac{1}{2}$" (1.9 cm) apart.

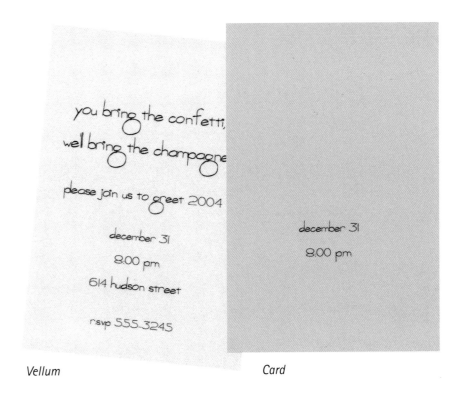

you bring the confetti,
we'll bring the champagne

please join us to greet 2004

december 31
8:00 pm
614 hudson street

r.s.v.p 555.3245

Vellum

december 31
8:00 pm

Card

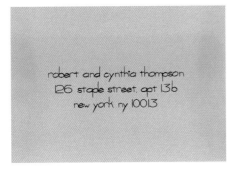

robert and cynthia thompson
126 staple street, apt 13b
new york ny 10013

Envelope

The gift tag, made from a place card, is tied to the present, creating a personalized element for all the friends and family on your Christmas mailing list. In PrintingPress, select everyone for whom you have a gift as "RSVP received," and change all the selected names to just first names or nicknames. The 3" x 4" (7.6 x 10.2 cm) card has one horizontal fold and is printed on both sides. The front has a red-and-white checkerboard border—a Platinum edition feature—around both the name and the imported snowman graphic. The standard table number information is changed to white so it won't be printed, and the inside greeting is typed on top of it.

Cynthia

Outside

Happy Holidays!

Love,
Aunt Tilly, Uncle Frank,
Cara and Todd

Inside

A mother's love determines how
We love ourselves and others.
There is no sky we'll ever see
Not lit by that first love.

Turlough O'Carolan

be mine

Please join me for a feast
on a blanket under a shady tree.

This Sunday, 11:00 a.m.

Prepare for a day of pampering
and, of course, brownies.

♥

I love you.

Robert

fete d'amour

Holidays of the Heart

Love letters are back. Although email may be taking over as the everyday means of communication, the electronic age has made paper-based correspondence a more treasured commodity.

Today's love letters don't need to be from a lover, written in longhand, and wrapped with a ribbon for safekeeping. Modern notes of affection can be made on the computer and sent to girlfriends, old high school pals—anyone who deserves more than just a virtual greeting. Here's how to make the real thing.

A DAY FOR LOVE

"Women always tend to care more about Valentine's Day than men do," says relationship expert Nancy Slotnick, who helps men and women find love on her website Cablight.com. "I would recommend sending valentines to all your single women friends. They are especially vulnerable and sad when they don't have a valentine. Knowing that your women friends love you can be the next best thing."

For your significant other, however, Nancy says a store-bought card is nice as long as your write your own words inside. "We don't have a lot of opportunities to say how we feel," she says. For her wedding, Nancy and her fiancée were asked by their rabbi to write down what they loved about one another. "Getting to see what my husband wrote and having the exercise of writing down my thoughts, that was a very powerful experience," Nancy says.

"It's really nice to express what you have to say in a card. There are a lot of things that you might want to tell the person you love but feel too vulnerable or embarrassed to say it out loud," says Nancy. "Writing it down might be easier, especially if you are the kind of person who has a hard time expressing yourself."

To express how you really feel, make a one-of-kind valentine on your computer. "A homemade card is especially good because it comes straight from the heart," says Nancy.

HELP FOR RELUCTANT WRITERS

For some, composing the card is the hardest part. For a jump-start, find poetry that means a lot to you, or consult a book of quotations. For a Mother's Day card, look under the topic of motherhood or family for inspiration. "Lyrics from a song are always really good," suggests Nancy. The exact words are easy to find on the Internet.

BE AN OFFICIAL ROMANTIC

If you're throwing a party for two, whether a romantic picnic or a weekend getaway, make an invitation. "Anything in writing adds an official touch," says Nancy. "There is a thought that you have to spend a lot of money to show your love, but I don't think that's the case. If you get creative and put thought into the details, it can be just as nice, if not nicer than spending a lot of money."

Nancy suggests creating a menu card filled with all your loved one's favorite foods. "Men tend to like that you are thinking about what things they like. If you write about some special memory you had together or put his favorite dessert on the menu, it's much more appreciated." Note the picnic invitation in the photo specifically mentions brownies will be served.

The Projects

This little valentine is perfect for slipping into a box of chocolates, wedging between a dozen long-stemmed roses, or hiding in a school lunch. Add a simple red heart graphic, scaled to the size of the paper, and print "be mine" in *Jackson Junior Wide* font. Print four to a page on white card stock cut to 4½" x 8" (11.4 x 20.3 cm) and trim to 2½" x 4" (5.7 x 10.2 cm). The envelope, originally intended for enclosure cards, measures 4½" x 2½" (10.8 x 6.4 cm). Design the envelope as an inner envelope so just the recipient's name is printed, not his or her entire address.

be mine

Valentine envelope

Please join me for a feast

on a blanket under a shady tree.

This Sunday, 11:00 a.m.

Prepare for a day o,

and, of course, b

Robert

Valentine card

to my darling Robert

♥

I love you.

Picnic envelope

Picnic invitation

The ivory stationery for the "picnic for two" invitation came as a stationery set and was personalized by adding a bright picnic graphic and the fun *Sky Pie* font to set the mood. Design the coordinating envelope as an inner envelope so only the recipient's name is printed.

For a Mother's Day card or Mother's Day brunch invitation, use a pink folded card, $8\frac{1}{2}$ x $5\frac{1}{2}$ (21.6 x 14 cm). Reprint a poem in a beautiful, feminine script font. As a card, the inside can be left blank, or print a simple "Happy Mother's Day." Don't forget to handwrite a thoughtful message to Mom. As an invitation to a brunch, print the details of the event inside the card in the same script font. Use the matching script font for the address and return address on the coordinating A2 envelope.

For a softer, more feminine touch, round the corners of the Mother's Day card with a corner punch, available at most office supply stores and craft stores.

A mother's love determines how
We love ourselves and others.
There is no sky we'll ever see
Not lit by that first love.

Turlough O'Carolan

Mother's Day invitation (outside)

Robert and Cynthia Thompson
826 Franklin Street
New York, New York 10002

Envelope

Please join us for a
Mother's Day Brunch
to honor our mothers

Sunday, May 10, 2004
eleven o'clock
614 Hudson Street

Regrets Only 555-1234

Mother's Day invitation (inside)

Zinfandel

Wine Tasting Notes

Swirl, Swish and Spit

Join us for a wine tasting party

Please bring your favorite bottle of wine.

Saturday, July 27
8:00 p.m.
125 North Main Street

R.S.V.P. 555-1234

David and Susan Adam

Riesling

Swirl, Swish and Spit

ten year

Martinis. Sinatra.
Need we say more?

Please join us for cocktails
Saturday, July 27
8:00 p.m.
614 Hudson Street

RSVP
555-

Feeling a bit blue?
We can fix that.

Please join us for cocktails
Saturday, July 27, 8:00 pm
125 North Main Street

RSVP 555-1234

hors d'oeuvres go so
nicely with cocktails

come see for yourself
Saturday, July 27, 8:00 pm
614 Hudson Street

R.S.V.P. 555-1234

chapter 5

for celebrations
and soirées

for a grape party

Wining with Friends

"There is no end to the number of themes you can create for a wine tasting," says Joshua Wesson, co-CEO of Best Cellars, a chain of wine stores that appeals to both wine experts and novices. "Wine from a specific region or country, wines that go with pizza, Chardonnays from around the world—the themes can be as prosaic or poetic as you care to make them."

WHAT'S THE RALLYING CRY?

If you are asking guests to bring wine for the tasting, you have to pick a theme early on. The theme will guide the type of wines your party will feature, so make sure you include on the invitations what type of wine your guests should bring, being as specific as you like. If you're a serious wine taster, make sure this is reflected in the invitation. If you're more experimental, your invitation can reflect the more playful aspects of wine tasting. Also, let people know if they should bring pillows and toothbrushes or if you will be arranging taxis for them to get home. "If you're planning a somewhat unusual or unfamiliar event, let your guests know what to expect. Not everyone likes surprises," says Megan.

If you are providing the wine, you can have more control over quantity and quality. "The magic number of wines to serve at a tasting is between six and ten," explains Joshua. "A tasting portion is about two ounces (56.7 g), a drinking por-tion is three to four ounces (85 to 113.4 g), and a bottle is generally twenty-five ounces (708.7 g)," says Joshua. Use this guide to determine how many bottles of wine you will need.

PREP SCHOOL

However the wine is getting to the party, make sure it arrives at the proper temper-ature for pouring. "Sticking a warm bottle of wine in the refrigerator won't chill it quickly enough, and you don't want to put it in the freezer. Inevitably you'll forget, the cork will explode, and you'll have Beaujolais all over your frozen turkey," warns Joshua. Plan on having a bucket of ice ready to keep the white wines chilled when your guests arrive.

It's a good idea to print out information about each wine to help your guests learn to distinguish the dif-ferent qualities. In this example, cards were

printed with the type of wine, but you can also include information about the vine-yard and the particular vintage.

If you want to assign each person a glass, purchase wine charms, or make tags using the PrintingPress place card feature. Create a 3" x 3" (7.6 x 7.6 cm) place card with no folds and the name printed along one of the edges. Print on card stock, and using a scissor, cut from the center of one side to the middle of the square, then cut or punch a small circle for the stem.

GET WITH THE PROGRAM

"It's a good idea to have a sheet of paper on which guests can write. The sheet should list each wine, the vintage, and its origin," advises Joshua. "You can put together some interesting background information from what you can glean from a web search."

Use PrintingPress to create a journal for each guest to keep track of his or her wine notes. Display them with a cup full of pens or pencils.

Zinfandel

Wine Tasting Notes

Swirl, Swish and Spit

Join us for a wine tasting party

Please bring your favorite botltle of wine.

Saturday, July 27
8:00 p.m.
125 North Main Street
R.S.V.P. 555-1234
David and Susan Adams

Riesling

Swirl, Swish and

The Projects

To announce the fall harvest theme of the party, the invitations arrived in bright-orange-speckled envelopes. The gold stationery contrasted with orange text written in an old-fashioned typewriter-style font.

The invitation was made using PrintingPress Platinum, which allows you to rotate text boxes. Swirl, Swish and Spit using a font named *Depot* was rotated 90 degrees to run along the left side of the 5" x 7" (12.7 x 17.8 cm) invitation with a $1\frac{1}{2}$" (3.2 cm) left margin. The envelope also has vertical text in the same font as the invitation and journal.

Envelope

Invitation card

The Wine Tasting Notes features the same text treatment as the invitation. The journal was created as a double-sided program, measuring 11" x 5½" (27.9 x 14 cm) when unfolded.

The wine labels are designed as 3½" x 4" (8.9 x 10.2 cm) folded note cards. The wine name is printed on both sides. PrintingPress automatically inverts the text and images on the "Outside Back" so it reads the correct way when printed.

Wine Tasting Notes

Suggested adjectives

Barnyardy	Fruity	Peppery
Bite	Grapey	
Perfumed	Bitter	Green
Smoky		
Buttery	Heady	Spicy
Chewy	Herbaceous	Sweet
Corked	Murky	Tart
Dirty	Musty	Toasty
Earthy	Oaky	Velvety
Flinty	Oxidized	Zesty

Wine journal (outside front)   *Wine journal (outside back)*

wine	look	smell	taste	wine	look	smell	taste
Abadia Retuerta 2001 Rivola Ribera del Duero, Spain				Anapamu 2001 Pinot Noir Central Coast, California			
Alamos 2001 Bonarda Argentina, South America				Allende 1999 Rioja Crianza Rioja, Spain			
Alderbrook 1999 Zinfandel Sonoma Valley, California							

Wine journal (inside)

through the years

Make Every Anniversary Golden

Most wedding anniversaries are celebrated in private with a special dinner or a vacation, but big milestone anniversaries such as the twenty-fifth and fiftieth deserve big parties. "These are most often surprise parties thrown by the couple's children," says Sherry Schweitzer of A Touch of Class. "I've also seen couples throw parties for themselves. And when they do, they go all out."

"It's always a nice touch to use the couple's original wedding photo for the invitation, but if it's a surprise party, this might be hard to maneuver," points out Sherry. If you do have access to an original wedding photo, your options are endless. Assuming the couple wasn't married recently, you will first need to scan the photo to create an electronic file. You can have this done at most copy centers. Be sure to bring a diskette or CD on which to save the electronic file. You can then import it into your PrintingPress projects.

If a photo is a significant part of the invitation, consider printing on glossy photo stock. Also, check if your printer has a special photo setting that will print your photos more crisply.

Don't despair if you can't procure a wedding photo—there are still plenty of options. "Just keep it simple. Find something pretty and light, or try to replicate the original wedding invitation from years ago," Sherry says.

Another idea is to focus on what kind of couple they are and what they like to do together. If they are big travelers, design the invitation as a passport, or create a theme of their favorite country, such as Italy. This theme will also help you decide what food to serve, wine to buy, and music to play.

"I'll ask whoever is throwing the party, 'What is this couple all about?'" says Sherry. "Sometimes you find a couple who loves to gamble. Then we pull out our roulette table and throw a casino night."

WHEN IT'S A SURPRISE

Surprise parties can be a lot of work, but when they work out, they're worth it. One of the biggest challenges is creating a guest list that will not cause post-party headaches for the honorees.

"For my parents' twenty-fifth wedding anniversary, my sisters and I decided to throw a party at a Chinese restaurant. I had a Bat Mitzvah a couple years earlier, so we had the invitation list from that to use. But inevitably, we ended up hurting someone's feelings by not inviting them," says Erica Busch, an attorney in New York City. "If it's just two more people you're not sure about, invite them," advises Erica. "But if those two then turn into another couple, then another, just don't invite the whole group."

It is important to let the guests know if the party is a surprise to the happy couple, so be sure to include the information on the invitation. "It's a great idea to come up with a cover story and let the guests be in on it from the very beginning," says Megan. "Everyone loves to be included in a secret, and the invitation is the perfect place to let people know that Mom and Dad think they're going to the movies."

GET WITH THE PROGRAM

Surprise or not, every anniversary party should have some kind of presentation or program. "We played a version of Jeopardy in which the categories were things about my parents," Erica says, "like vacations, ailments, and my father's favorite foods. All the guests played and had fun laughing at things my parents have done and said over the years."

You can easily facilitate such a game by printing cards with trivia questions about

thank you thank you thank
you thank you thank you
thank you thank you
thank you thank you
thank you thank you
thank you thank you
thank you thank you thank
you thank you thank you

It's hard to believe
that it has already
been ten years!
Join us as we
cele brate
our love
Saturday, December 13
eight o'clock pm
125 North Main St

R   S   V   P
5 5 5 - 1 2 1 2

songs from 1993
blast from the
the past
songs from
1993 blast
from the
past songs
from 1993
blast from the past

Love
egan
1993

the couple, even including photos as questions or clues. The married couple will enjoy not only hearing everyone struggle to answer the questions but hearing the questions that you came up with as well.

Programs, whether they are songs, poems, slideshows, or games, are a terrific way to personalize a party. "The program is your chance to make your party stand out. You don't have to be fancy; you just have to be creative," says Erica. "If you have no talent as a singer, that just makes it funnier."

If you do plan a theatrical program, it deserves a paper program to go along with it. Include the same photo or graphic that was used on the invitation, and give all the performers proper credit. It's also a great place to let all the guests know why a particular song is special to the couple, or what inspired the skit performed in their honor.

NAME THAT TUNE

Music is the best time machine, so why not make a CD with all the couple's favorite tunes as a party favor? You can include their photo on the CD label as well as their wedding date and the current date to celebrate the number of years that have passed. Playing the CD during the party might even lure Mom and Dad onto the dance floor.

The Project

To create this project, use the same design in different sizes for all the pieces, including the invitation, thank-you note, and CD cover.

Using PrintingPress Platinum, place a photo in the center and position justified text around it. Create one text box to cover the entire card, and leave space in the middle for the photo. Make a second text box for the blank space to the right of the photo and a third box for the space to the left.

For the airy, modern spacing of the lettering, use the Condense/Expand Vertically tool in the text box window. Make the font in all three text boxes the same point size and color, so it looks like continuous text.

When working with the photo, try converting it to grayscale, even if it was a color photo, to create a more classic look and enhance the sense of history that the couple is celebrating. Select a dark gray for the text color to soften the look on the glossy photo paper when printed.

CD jewel case

CD label

It's hard to believe
that it has alre
been ten yea
Join   u
a   s   w
cele   br
o u r   l
Saturday, December
eight o'clock
125 North Main St

R   S   V   P
5 5 5 - 1 2 1 2

Invitation card

Robert and Cynthia Thompson
826 Franklin Street
New York, NY 10002

Envelope

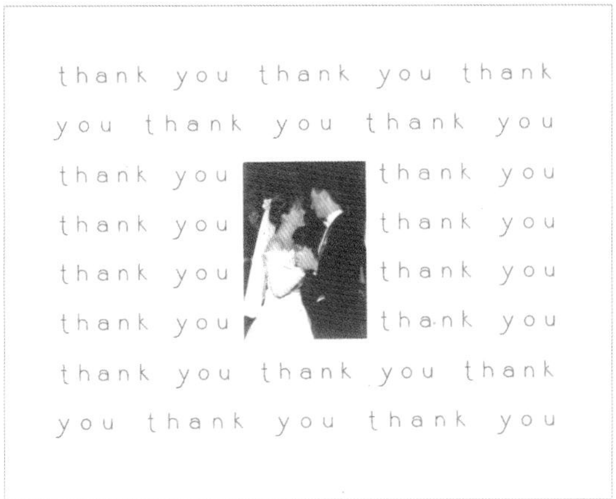

thank you thank you thank
you thank you thank you
thank you   thank you
thank you   thank you
thank you   thank you
thank you   thank you
thank you thank you thank
you thank you thank you

Folded thank-you note

Martinis. Sinatra.
Need we say more?

Please join us for cocktails
Saturday, July 27
8.00 p.m.
614 Hudson Street

R.S.V.P.
555...

Feeling a bit blue?
We can fix that.

Please join us for cocktails
Saturday July 27, 8.00 p.m.
125 North Main Street

R.S.V.P. 555 1234

Emma & Andrew
614 Hudson St
New York, N...

hors d'oeuvres go so
nicely with cocktails

come see for yourself
saturday, July 27, 8:00 p.m.
614 Hudson Street

R.S.V.P. 555-1234

with a twist

Shaking It Up

Cocktail parties are the perfect solution for when you have the itch to entertain but you're tight on time. By making invitations on your computer, you can whip together a party in less time than it takes to dig out the blender.

  "If you have the time and inclination to send an invitation by snail mail, go for it," says Allana Baroni, author of *Flirtini: A Guide to Mixing and Mingling.* "When guests receive an invitation by mail, they tend to take the party more seriously. A group email suggests: Kegger! A handmade invite suggests: Special event!"

WHAT'LL IT BE?

Cocktail parties—hip and retro at the same time—are purely about having fun, so make sure you have fun creating the invitations as well. Our invitations all use images of cocktails, but you can incorporate other elements. "Poking a bamboo umbrella through an invitation really starts the party mood," says Megan. "With our busy schedules and heavy work loads, we're all excited at the thought of relaxing and having fun with friends."

"When I lived in New York City, my roommates and I decided to kick off the summer with a cocktail party called 'Hamptons Whine and Jersey Cheez' in honor of the two local beach locations and their rival reputations," says Joan Buyce, a Boston native who favors the Jersey shore. "We asked our guests to bring whatever they identified with. It was an instant conversation starter."

Joan's invitation also made it clear to her guests she was serving only wine and cheese, which helped her plan her budget. Another idea is to serve a signature drink, such as a mojito or cosmopolitan. Decide this ahead of time so you can include a graphic or special instructions on your invitation. For example, if you love martinis but don't have a set of martini glasses, ask that everyone bring one single glass. Once the party is over you'll have an eclectic collection through which to remember the party and your friends.

The Projects

All three invitations were created using martini graphics and text. For the Sinatra invitation, the text was centered under the martini graphic, included in the PrintingPress software and printed on plain white card stock. The same martini image was added to a white envelope.

Martinis. Sinatra.

Need we say more?

Please join us for cocktails

Saturday, July 27

8:00 p.m.

125 North Main Street

R.S.V.P.
555-1234

Sinatra invitation

Robert and Cynthia Thompson
126 Staple Street, Apt 13B
New York, NY 10013

Sinatra envelope

The blue martini invitation was made with PrintingPress Platinum, which allows you to float images so they can be easily positioned anywhere on the page. The blue martini graphic, included in PrintingPress Platinum, floats on the right side of the card. For more about floating images, turn to Chapter Seven, "Tools & Techniques."

Blue martini envelope

Feeling a bit blue?
We can fix that.

Please join us for cocktails
Saturday, July 27, 8:00 p.m.
125 North Main Street

R.S.V.P. 555 1234

Blue martini invitation

hors d'oeuvres go so
nicely with cocktails

come see for yourself
Saturday, July 27, 8:00 p.m.
614 Hudson Street

R.S.V.P. 555-1234

Four martini invitation

The invitation with four martini glasses was also made with PrintingPress Platinum. The martini glass graphic was copied and pasted three times. Each martini glass was then recolored by adjusting its hue and brightness. The Recolor Image tool is located in the Image menu, and also appears as a color wheel on the toolbar. For more about recoloring photos and graphics, turn to Chapter Seven, "Tools & Techniques." The font *Inkburrow*, designed by Uddi Uddi, lends a chic and mod style to the invitation.

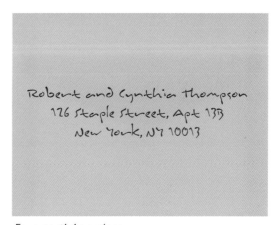

Four martini envelope

guess who's coming to dinner?

Party of Four ... or More

Erika Lenkert, author of *The Last-Minute Party Girl: Fashionable, Fearless and Foolishly Simple Entertaining,* has found that having dinner parties has recently become more popular. "People want good food, comfort food, not big, opulent parties," she said. "Everything is way more relaxed; we're not serving fancy, sculptured meals."

Erika has also noticed hosts are being more creative and making their parties more personalized. Creating invitations is one way to do so. "Hosts are looking for invitations that have the personality and energy of their party," says Erika. "They don't want cookie-cutter invitations."

For a relaxed host who favors simplicity but is seeking individuality, a great-looking invitation made on a home computer is the answer. "It's somewhere between the very formal and the very informal."

WHAT TO SAY

"The words you choose are really important when creating invitations," says Erika, who in her book compares a party invitation to an advertisement for a movie. "Get creative with every detail. You could say 'dinner' but you could also say 'feast' to make it more exciting."

Be very clear about what kind of party you're having so your guests know what to wear and what to expect. Erika stresses being specific. "If you want them to bring wine, tell them," she says. If you're having any kind of theme or activity, here's your chance to let it be known. If you're expecting costumes at your Halloween party, make it clear so you're not the only one in an Austin Powers suit.

SET THE TONE

"Details such as the invitation and the place cards are a great way to tie everything together," says Deborah Fabricant, celebrity party planner. "The invitation will set the tone for the party; how you set the table will help carry it out." For a holiday party, you don't have to go overboard decking your halls or turning your home red and green. Use the poinsettia image on the invitation, add it to the menu and place cards, and find just a few hearty poinsettia plants for centerpieces.

When designing your invitation, think about what you will be serving. You don't need to have your whole menu figured out, but if it's going to be barbecue, you'll want to convey that in your invitation so your guests can figure out what they can bring to complement your meal. This will also give them clues for how to dress. Don't forget to include the most reachable way for your guests to RSVP. If you never have your cell phone turned on, don't offer that number. Make sure you include the date and location of the party, and print an extra invitation for your scrapbook.

Good directions or a map is always appreciated in an invitation. Once the party starts, you don't want to have to deal with getting lost party-goers to your door. Look up your address on a website that offers driving directions. Find main roads from all points to offer your guests.

Please join us for dinner

Saturday, August 10

7:00 p.m.

614 Hudson Street

R.S.V.P. 555-1234
Emma and Andrew Foster

Robert and Cynthia Thompson
826 Franklin Street
New York, New York 10002

Asparagus-Parmesan Cheese Puffs

Maine Crab Cakes

Blini with Caviar & Creme Fraiche

. . .

Beef Braised in Red Wine

Roasted Asparagus with Lemon

Potato and Onion Gratin

. . .

Valrhona Chocolate Creme Brulee

Mango and Pineapple Sorbet

Cynthia

The Project

In the example, we used letterpress stationery by Studio Z Mendocino, which includes invitations and envelopes, menus, and place cards.

The invitation shown is 5" x 7" (12.7 x 17.8 cm) and fits into an A7 envelope. The stationery is designed to the size of the card, and the margins are set to avoid printing over the existing letterpress graphics on the stationery. When designing invitations on paper with preprinted graphics, it's important to find a font style that coordinates with the design and further communicates the type of dinner party you are planning.

Once you've sent out the invitations and your guests start calling to RSVP, keep track by entering their responses into your PrintingPress mailing list. This way, you can start designing your place cards.

Please join us for dinner

Saturday, August 10

7:00 p.m.

614 Hudson Street

R.S.V.P. 555-1234
Emma and Andrew Foster

Robert and Cynthia Thompson
826 Franklin Street
New York, New York 10002

Asparagus-Parmesan Cheese Puffs

Maine Crab Cakes

Blini with Caviar & Creme Fraiche

. . .

Beef Braised in Red Wine

Roasted Asparagus with Lemon

Potato and Onion Gratin

. . .

Valrhona Chocolate Creme Brulee

Mango and Pineapple Sorbet

If you plan to seat your guests around one table, you'll want to create a one-sided place card. Decide if you want the guests' full name, or if you want to make it more casual by just using first names. In PrintingPress, whatever appears in the status dialog box of your guest will be on the place cards. To change a name, select the guest's name and click the Edit button. For more information about printing place cards, please see Chapter Seven, "Tools & Techniques."

The last thing to create is your menu card. You don't want to print a menu featuring grilled salmon only to get to the store and choose filet of sole. Also, if any of your guests would like to bring a dish, you can give them credit on the menu, such as writing "Aunt Lucile's sweet potatoes." Unless your party is very formal, have fun with it.

chapter 6

for in-between parties

stationery of your very own

Letter Perfect

Kathy Reuter didn't let the St. Louis snowstorms slow her down this past winter. "We were snowed in, so I've kept busy making stationery," says the third-grade teacher. "I've made at least 150 sets of stationery for friends and family."

Each of the thirty teachers with whom Kathy works received a pack of twenty sheets of personalized stationery. "At first I was using their first names, but then a friend pointed out that I should use what the students call them, so they can use them as thank-you notes," she says. She also personalized the stationery: For her friend who loves to garden, she added a topiary. For her younger colleagues, she used the red shoe. "I think I've used every PrintingPress font and every graphic. Everyone was so happy to get something so personal."

"Personalized accessories are always in good taste," says Megan "Whether it's a canvas tote or a note card, when your name or initials are there, it becomes distinctive and special. Right now, for example, it's trendy to have a monogram or initial on a purse or a sweater."

Monograms, the combination of a person's three initials or a couple's first initials and last initial, have been around for a long time. Legend dates them back to King Charlemagne who was said to be illiterate and, therefore, signed important documents with his initials. Some sources credit the origin of the monogram simply as laundry markers for keeping linens straight, whereas others say artists and printers were first to use monograms to sign their work.

"Monograms offer an old-world, Victorian feel. People gravitate to that in this digital age," says Megan. "Monogramming every-day items such as slippers or bathrobes increases their perceived value because traditionally only very expensive items would be engraved with a monogram."

TAKE IT PERSONALLY

Monograms, whether they adorn a dress shirt cuff, crystal, or stationery, can be designed in an infinite number of ways. Elaborate monograms may have initials shaped into a drawing of an animal or flower; traditional monograms use a script type and may have an oval or diamond border.

Typically, monograms are designed with the middle character slightly larger than the initials on either side. For an individual, the surname is in the middle position, flanked on either side by the first and middle initial. For a married couple, the surname initial is traditionally placed between her first initial on the left and his on the right. Individuals who would like their initials read in order of first, middle, and last should keep all the letters the same size.

For example, Sylvia Ann Jones would create a monogram as SJA. If Sylvia were to marry Tom Lewis and take his last name, their married monogram would appear as SLT. If she were to keep her given name, they might use both their last initials with a hyphen or design in between, such as J~L.

To create a monogram in this fashion, use the monogram tool offered in PrintingPress Platinum. The tool can use any font to create a monogram that exactly captures your personality. The tool also allows you to size the side letters and adjust their overlap of the center initial. To read more about monograms, turn to Chapter Seven, "Tools & Techniques."

A Guide to Personalized Stationery

The type of paper and envelope you use for any communication is a reflection of you and the message you are sending. Although it may be obvious that a thank-you note for a job interview should be written on quality paper, there are actually quite a few more details besides paper quality to consider when creating personalized stationery.

This guide helps demystify and define the many standard types of personalized stationery so you can start thinking about what's right for you. Your name, initial, or monogram should be printed on the stationery, and your return address should be printed on the envelope. You can be creative with paper colors and textures, choice of fonts and ink color, and placement of your name, initial, or monogram on the stationery.

Regardless of size or shape, it's best to handwrite the note, even if your penmanship looks more like chicken scratch than prose. Just write as neatly as possible and avoid cross-outs by planning what you are going to write before your pen hits the paper. Business correspondence can be typed, though handwritten notes of gratitude and quick thoughts present a nice, personal touch.

Keep in mind, most of the following sizes are approximate. When creating stationery, start with the envelope sizes first; you can always trim paper to fit. The placement and inclusion of names and addresses on the different types of stationery vary from source to source, so use the following descriptions as a suggestion for your design. Let your own needs, style, and taste dictate your personalized stationery. After all, it should be personal.

Common Cards

CORRESPONDENCE CARDS WITH COORDINATING ENVELOPES

Correspondence cards are generally a nice quality card stock with the approximate dimensions of 4" x 6" (10.2 x 15.2 cm). When personalized, a full name or monogram appears in the top-left corner or center of the card. Often a border is used around the card in the same color ink as the name. These cards can be used to show gratitude for a dinner party or a gift. They are also used for general social correspondence. The coordinating envelope should have the address on the back flap.

HALF SHEETS

A half sheet is also quality stationery that's approximately 7" x 10" (17.8 x 25.4 cm), though some use a smaller version half sheet of 5" x 7" (12.7 x 17.8 cm). A monogram or name, or name and address, are printed at the top, and the handwritten note begins under the name. If the paper is of a thick weight, you can write on the back of the page. If more pages are needed, the writing continues on a blank version of the stationery for the second page. The paper is folded in half with the printed name on the outside. The fold is inserted in the envelope first, so the corners of the page are on top.

FOLD-OVER NOTES

Some consider this card the most formal type of social stationery. Unfolded, the card is usually about 5" x7" (12.7 x 17.8 cm). The fold is most often at the top, with the name or monogram centered on the front. Writing begins on the inside and continues on the inside front. Messages should not be continued on the back. Small versions of these cards are called informals.

Business Paper

BUSINESS LETTERHEAD

Business letterhead is always on $8\frac{1}{2}$" x 11" (21.6 x 27.9 cm) sheets of paper in the United States; and 210 x 297 mm ($8\frac{1}{4}$" x $11\frac{7}{100}$"), in the United Kingdom and should include all available contact information, such as address, phone number, fax number, email, and website. It can also include the name and title of the person using the stationery. The stationery is folded into thirds before being placed into an envelope. Most often, the return address on the envelope is on the front.

MONARCH

Created with a piece of 7" x 10" (17.8 x 25.4 cm) paper, monarch notes include the name and title at the top, are folded into thirds, and fit in a coordinating envelope with the return address on the back. Monarch notes are more informal than letterhead. These notes, without any business name or title, are often used for social correspondence as well.

Everything Else

LETTER SHEETS

The proliferation of email has lessened the demand for everyday stationery such as letter sheets. Typically, letter sheets have a name, address, and phone number printed on the top and plenty of space for a longer note. Letter sheets are often used less for pure social reasons and more for personal business inquiries.

CALLING CARDS

Much like a business card, a social calling card is a 2" x 3" (5.1 x 7.6 cm) heavy card that provides all the necessary contact information for getting in touch with its holder. They can also be used as a reminder or a gift enclosure.

HOUSE STATIONERY

A remnant of the era of estates and plantations, house stationery is now used for anyone who may own more than one home. The name and/or address of the home is printed at the top or on the front of the stationery.

WHAT'S IN A NAME?

Initials and monograms are just one way to design beautiful personalized stationery. Using one's full name offers many creative options.

"The font is really important when using your name on your stationery," says Megan. "It really needs to capture your style."

Type your name into PrintingPress, and copy and paste it several times. Choose a different font for each one to see what type of feeling it conveys. If one font seems very casual and fun, try using it with your nickname, or just your first name, and putting it on a larger piece of stationery. If a font is very formal, it may be well suited for a folded note card with your first, middle, and last names.

"Don't forget that you can add graphics, too," says Megan. "A cute little purse in the corner of a note card or a sailboat above your name can add more interest to the stationery and can further communicate your style. In general, resize graphics so they are fairly small to keep the look clean, sophisticated, and uncluttered."

A GIFT THAT WILL DEFINITELY FIT

Personalized stationery makes a wonderful gift for newly engaged couples, a host, a new parent, or members of a wedding party. Creating the stationery on your computer allows you to make an assortment of designs that can be beautifully packaged and will be wonderfully received.

"I took a few reams of card stock to a photocopy place, and for next to nothing, they cut it to the size I wanted. I bought colored envelopes in bulk, and keep it all on hand," says Kathy. "Then it's all about the packaging. I bought beautiful ribbon and put every set in cellophane bags. Everyone was so impressed. My principal has called me twice to ask for more."

THE SHAPE OF THINGS

The first thing to consider when designing personalized stationery is whether you prefer a flat card or folded note. Folded notes are traditionally used as thank-you notes; flat cards are more popular for general correspondence. If you're making a gift for someone and not sure of his or her taste, try an assortment of each.

STATIONERY	NAME	FEEL	USED FOR
FOLDED NOTE	FULL NAME	FORMAL	THANK-YOU NOTES
SMALL CARD	FIRST NAME OR NICKNAME AND LAST NAME	CASUAL	CORRESPONDENCE
4" x 9" (10.2 x 22.9 CM)	FIRST NAME AND GRAPHIC	FUN	QUICK NOTES, LISTS
LETTER	FULL NAME	CORPORATE	BUSINESS

The Projects

White stationery was paired with a lime green translucent envelope. The card is 5" x 7" (12.7 x 17.8 cm) and features lime green ink to match the envelope. One of PrintingPress's original fonts, *Jackson Junior Sans Wide*, was used in all lowercase for a modern, informal look.

emma foster

emma foster
614 hudson street
new york, ny 10029

Vellum envelope

Flat card

The red paper and envelope came as a stationery set and was easily customized by adding a monogram. The paper and envelopes are custom sizes, so the dimensions were entered into PrintingPress by choosing *New Stationery* from the *Stationery* menu and then entering the unfolded card size into the *Layout* page.

Envelope

Flat card with monogram

For the folded note with a single initial, a cursive font was used. The color of the E is designed to match the coordinating, darker envelope. Whenever you use a colored ink on colored paper, make sure you have extra pieces of the paper so you can test the result before the final print. Make sure to print in ink that is darker than the paper color so it stands out.

Envelope

Emma Foster
614 Hudson Street
New York, NY 10029

In all stationery samples, a return address is printed on the back of the envelope. The return address is designed with the same font and color as the personalization on the stationery. To print the envelope return addresses using PrintingPress, create the envelope as a "reply" envelope and select *Print backs only* in the *Print* window.

Folded initial card

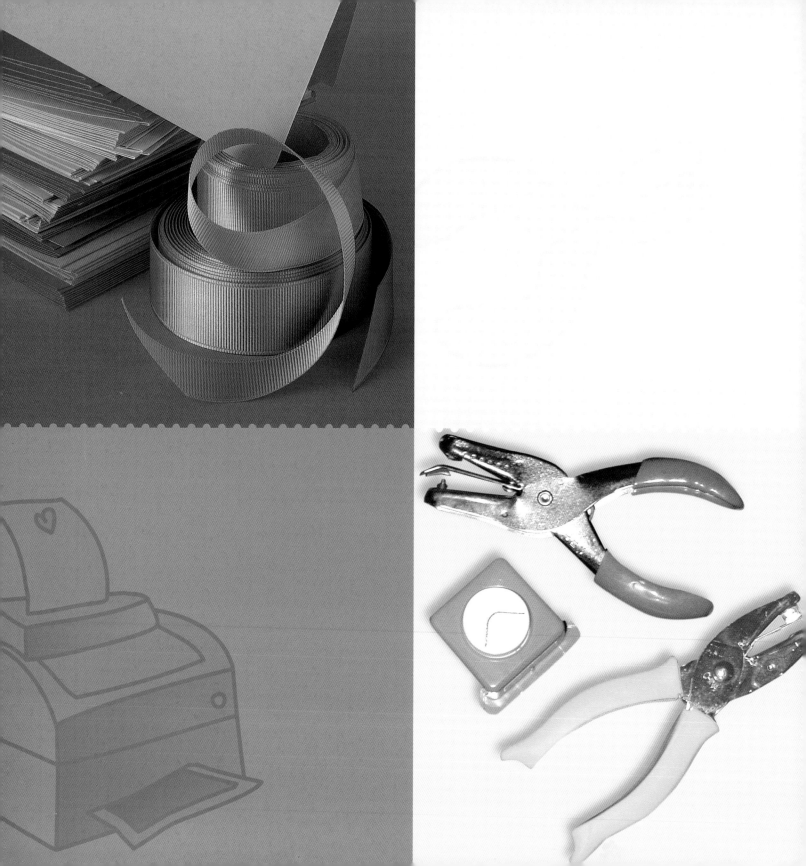

chapter 7

tools & techniques

a guide to invitation stationery

Choosing Your Materials

Depending on your budget and resources, your choices of paper are endless. The Internet offers dozens of websites devoted exclusively to affordable, printer-compatible stationery, and many websites will mail you paper samples upon request. The benefits of shopping in a stationery store include the ability to browse, see exact colors, and feel paper textures and weights.

Whether shopping virtually or in a store, it's best to know how to use words to describe paper. Paper used for invitations is often referred to as "card stock," but this can mean a wide variety of weights. Generally speaking, plain paper is called "text weight" and is measured in pounds written with the pound sign, such that 24 pound paper would be written as 24#. In countries using the metric system, this measurement is in grams per square meter and would be written as 90.3 gsm or g/m². Heavier paper may be called "index weight," or "cardstock," and the heaviest paper is called "cover stock." Most printer-compatible stationery is no heavier than 80#, or 218.22 gsm, cover stock. Some manufacturers make very heavy-weight panel cards that are compatible with certain printers, but you should buy a small quantity to test before you buy enough for a large project.

Paper also comes in various textures and finishes and is made from various materials. Cover stock used for cards is typically made from wood pulp and is bleached white with a smooth finish. Cards can also be made from cotton and other fibers, with various textured finishes, including "laid," which has stripes of texture, and "linen," which has a grid of texture. Textured paper absorbs ink differently and can cause it to bleed too much to be useful for photos, so glossy photo cards or smooth cover stock are often best for printing photos. Semitransparent material used for overlays is typically called "vellum," which can usually be printed on only with a laser printer, because the vellum does not absorb the ink from an ink-jet printer.

DETERMINING PAPER SIZE

When determining paper size, it's best to start by choosing envelopes and working backward. It's almost impossible—or at least very expensive—to make custom-sized envelopes, but you can always trim the paper to fit inside. Don't despair if the envelope doesn't match the paper you like—you can often get away with a "coordinating" envelope. It looks much better than one that almost matches (but not quite).

PAPER TYPE	FINISH	USES	PRINTER
COVER STOCK	SMOOTH	GENERAL PURPOSE	INK-JET OR LASER
COVER STOCK	LAID	SOPHISTICATED LOOK	INK-JET OR HIGH-END LASER
COVER STOCK	LINEN	BUSINESS STATIONERY	INK-JET OR HIGH-END LASER
COVER STOCK	GLOSSY	PHOTOS	INK-JET OR HIGH-END LASER
COVER STOCK	METALLIC	TRENDY LOOKS	LASER
COTTON	SOFT TEXTURE	CLASSIC LOOK	INK-JET
VELLUM	SHEEN	OVERLAYS	USUALLY LASER

The tables on the right list commonly used standard U.S. envelopes, and the corresponding paper size follows. Of course, what fits inside can vary depending on folds and shapes. European sizes are completely different, and high-end paperies often stock European papers because of their variety of colors and textures.

The United Kingdom's standard sizes are all based on the A series, starting with A1 measuring 594 x 841 mm. Each subsequent smaller size is half of the size larger, so the A2 is 420 x 594 mm. The most common size is the A4, which is the closest to the U.S. standard $8\frac{1}{2}$" x 11" sheet of paper. The C series is the coordinating envelopes to the A sizes.

DETERMINING POSTAL REQUIREMENTS

As of October 2004, a standard letter in the United States weighing up to 1 ounce (28.3 g) is $0.37. Each additional ounce is another $0.23. Postcards are required to be a minimum of $3\frac{1}{2}$" x 5" (8.9 x 12.7 cm) and a maximum of $4\frac{1}{4}$" x 6" (10.8 x 15.2 cm) and cost $0.23 to mail.

An additional $0.12 is charged for envelopes that are square, have clasps, strings, or buttons, or have an address parallel to its shorter side. Letters with enclosures that cause the thickness of the envelope to be uneven are also subject to an extra fee. Check with your local post office to ensure the correct postage before mailing.

In the United Kingdom, second-class mail aims to deliver letters within three business days. Letters up to 60g cost 21p. For letters to be delivered faster, they must be sent first class, which costs 28p for up to 60g.

U.S. ENVELOPE	CORRESPONDING PAPER SIZE
A2	$4\frac{1}{4}$" x $5\frac{1}{2}$" (10.8 x 14 CM) FLAT OR $8\frac{1}{2}$" x $5\frac{1}{2}$" (21.6 x 14 CM) FOLDED
A6	$4\frac{1}{2}$" x $6\frac{1}{4}$" (11.4 x 15.9 CM)
A7	5" x 7" (12.7 x 17.8 CM) FLAT OR 10" x 7" (25.4 x 17.8 CM) FOLDED
A8 (OUTER ENVELOPE)	$5\frac{1}{4}$" x $7\frac{3}{4}$" (13.3 x 19.7 CM)
4 BAR (BARONIAL)	$3\frac{1}{2}$" x 5" (8.9x 12.7 CM) FLAT OR 5" x 7" (12.7 x 17.8 CM) FOLDED
#10	4" x 9" (10.2 x 22.9 CM) FLAT OR $8\frac{1}{2}$" x 11" (21.6 x 27.9 CM) TRIFOLD
SQUARE	FROM 5" x 5" (12.7 x 12.7 CM) TO $9\frac{1}{2}$" x $9\frac{1}{2}$" (24.1 x 24.1 CM)

A SERIES FORMATS		C SERIES FORMATS	
A4	210 x 297 MM	C4	229 x 324 MM
A5	148 x 210 MM	C5	162 x 229 MM
A6	105 x 148 MM	C6	114 x 162 MM
A7	74 x 105 MM	C7	81 x 114 MM
A8	52 x 74 MM	C8	57 x 81 MM
A9	37 x 52 MM	C9	40 x 57 MM
A10	26 x 37 MM	C10	28 x 40 MM

U.S./IMPERIAL PAPERS	INCHES	MM
EXECUTIVE	$7\frac{1}{4}$ x $10\frac{1}{2}$	184 x 267
FOLIO/F4	$8\frac{1}{2}$ x 13	210 x 330
FOOLSCAP E	8 x 13	203 x 330
INDEX CARD	5 x 8	127 x 203
LEDGER	17 x 11	432 x 279
LEGAL	$8\frac{1}{2}$ x 14	216 x 356
LETTER (U.S.), A (ANSI A)	$8\frac{1}{2}$ x 11	216 x 279
PHOTO	4 x 6	102 x 152
QUARTO	$8\frac{1}{2}$ x $10\frac{13}{16}$	216 x 275
STATEMENT/HALFLETTER	$5\frac{1}{2}$ x $8\frac{1}{2}$	140 x 216
TABLOID (U.S.), B (ANSI B)	11 x 17	279 x 432

CUTTING, SCORING, PUNCHING

One of the most inexpensive ways to make your own invitations is to buy a ream of card stock and trim it to the appropriate size. If you are planning to make folds, you will need to score the paper first for a clean and professional-looking crease. For the best results, purchase the following tools from a stationery, art supply, office supply, or craft store:

ROTARY CUTTER—This tool cuts through paper as its circular blade is rolled. Some models allow you to replace the blade with decorative, perforating, or scoring blades. Rotary cutters have a ruler grid that enable you to measure and make straight cuts every time.

HOLE PUNCH—When attaching overlays or embellishments such as ribbons, it helps to have a selection of hole punches in different shapes and sizes. Wide ribbons need a large, rectangular hole, but thinner ribbons will not stay in place unless the hole is small.

CORNER PUNCH—A simple punch makes subtle, rounded corners, but more decorative versions are also available.

Our wedding weekend

BONE FOLDER—This tool, made of bone, can smooth, score, or crease paper.

DECORATIVE EDGER—Craft stores carry tools for creating scalloped edges and other effects. Add decorative edges after printing.

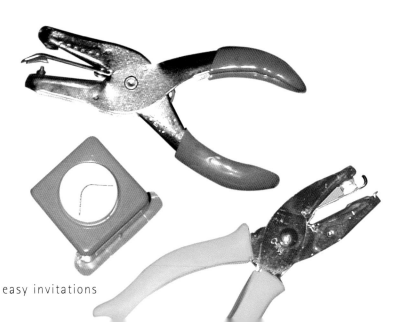

CHOOSING INK COLOR

The color ink you chose depends mostly on the color of the paper you are using. Before commiting to black ink on a white or ecru card, try out a dark blue, brown, or gray text color for a slight variation. If your paper is light green, make the text a dark shade of green for a subtle contrast. Always make sure the text ink color is dark enough and contrasts enough with the paper color to be legible.

Coordinate the ink color on your envelopes to match the ink color on your cards. If your envelopes are a different color from the invitations, or if they have a lining with another color, try matching the text color to this accent color to coordinate the two pieces. You can also choose an ink color to match any graphics or borders you are printing on the card.

SELECTING A FONT OR TYPEFACE

The font or typeface you choose should reflect the tone of the invitation. Fonts are divided into two main categories: Serif fonts, such as Jackson Junior, have "tails" on the ends of the letters; sans serif fonts, such as *Beckles*, do not. Generally, sans serif fonts are more modern, and serif fonts are more classic. You can mix the two, but don't exceed more than two or three fonts per invitation, and avoid mixing similar-looking fonts. The purpose of combining fonts is to show the contrasts between scripts and blocks, feminine and masculine.

You can achieve numerous effects by using different sizes and styles of the same font in a single invitation. Font sizes are measured in points, which are $\frac{1}{72}$ of an inch (.4 mm). Often you can make the names of the guests of honor stand out by using a larger point size of the same font as the rest of the invitation. You can also use a heavy or bold version of the font to emphasize someone's name. Finally, you can use alignment (left, right, center, or fully justified) to change the entire look and feel of the invitation while keeping the typeface the same.

CHOOSING A PRINTER

The two main types of printer available today are ink-jet and laser. Modern ink-jet printers transfer tiny droplets of ink onto the paper to create full-color images. They dry very quickly and typically will not smudge unless they get wet. They can print well onto any absorbent surface. Photo-quality ink-jet printers use six ink colors—cyan, magenta, yellow, black, light cyan, and light magenta—to blend skin tones better than four-color CMYK process.

Laser printers roll toner onto the surface of the paper and bind it to the paper with a hot roller called a fuser. They can achieve very fine strokes for script typefaces and can print on paper that is not absorbent, including vellum, but the toner may not fuse well to roughly textured papers. To blend grays or colors, laser printers use a halftone process, which resembles the look of a printed magazine page when viewed very closely.

	COLOR PHOTO INK-JET	BLACK-AND-WHITE LASER	COLOR LASER
COST	VERY LOW	MODERATE	HIGH
COST PER PRINT	HIGHEST	LOWEST	LOW COST/COLOR PRINT
SMUDGE	WHEN WET	TEXTURED PAPER	NONE
BEST AT	PHOTOS	FINE TEXT	GREAT QUALITY, HIGH VOLUME
COLOR MIXING	BLENDS INK COLORS	HALFTONE, GRAYS	HALFTONE, COLORS
COLORS AVAILABLE	C, M, Y, K, LC, LM	K	C, M, Y, K

a guide to wedding invitation wording

Choosing the color, font, size, and style of your wedding invitations might seem like a piece of cake compared to composing the actual text, especially if you come from a blended family.

Use the following suggestions for the scenario closest to yours. For traditional invitations, the best way to start is to follow this formula:

Basic Formula

INVITATIONAL LINE

REQUEST LINE

BRIDE'S NAME

JOINING WORD

GROOM'S NAME

DATE LINE

YEAR LINE

TIME LINE

LOCATION

CITY, STATE

In addition to making sure you have included all the necessary information for getting your guests to your wedding—and spelled everything correctly—it is just as important to be sure that no one's feelings will be hurt. When in doubt, check with all parties, and have the necessary conversations before the invitations are printed. It's better to fall short on tradition than on someone's feelings.

OTHER GENERAL RULES TO KEEP IN MIND

Be consistent.

If you are using Mr. and Mrs. for one set of parents, use it for everyone.

If you are spelling out the date, spell out all numbers. The year is not essential to include. Times are written in lowercase.

If you are using the British spelling of honour, use favour for the reply card.

Check titles. Titles such as Junior should be spelled out and preceded by a comma. However, long names or less formal invitations can use a "Jr." A "II" doesn't need a comma, but one can be used.

Know the religious differences. Weddings that take place outside a place of worship commonly use "request the pleasure of your company." Weddings that occur in a religious setting can read "request the honor of your presence." Also, many religions have different nuances; for example, Jewish weddings use the word "and" to join the bride and groom's names instead of "to". Check with your officiant to see if there is a preferred wording for the religious style you want to follow.

Represent your day. Even if the wording follows the proper format, it might not convey the style of your wedding. Be sure to choose words that describe the formality or spirit of your wedding day.

Traditional

MR. AND MRS. STUART FOSTER

REQUEST THE HONOR OF YOUR PRESENCE

AT THE MARRIAGE OF THEIR DAUGHTER

EMMA MARIE

TO

MR. WALTER CHRISTOPHER HOUGH

SATURDAY, THE EIGHTEENTH OF JUNE

TWO THOUSAND AND FOUR

AT SIX O'CLOCK

GREENACRES COUNTRY CLUB

SOMERSET, NEW JERSEY

Bride's family hosting

MRS. LYNNE SYLVIA FOSTER

AND

MR. STUART KEITH FOSTER

REQUEST THE HONOR OF YOUR PRESENCE

AT THE MARRIAGE OF THEIR DAUGHTER

EMMA MARIE

TO

MR. WALTER CHRISTOPHER HOUGH

SATURDAY, THE EIGHTEENTH OF JUNE

TWO THOUSAND AND FOUR

AT SIX O'CLOCK

GREENACRES COUNTRY CLUB

SOMERSET, NEW JERSEY

Divorced parents hosting

EMMA MARIE

DAUGHTER OF

STUART FOSTER AND THE LATE MEREDITH FOSTER

AND

WALTER CHRISTOPHER HOUGH

SON OF THEODORE AND HARRIET HOUGH

REQUEST THE HONOR OF YOUR PRESENCE

AT THEIR MARRIAGE

SATURDAY, THE EIGHTEENTH OF JUNE

TWO THOUSAND AND FOUR

AT SIX O'CLOCK

GREENACRES COUNTRY CLUB

SOMERSET, NEW JERSEY

One parent is deceased, remaining parent hosting, Version One

---

EMMA MARIE

DAUGHTER OF

STUART FOSTER AND MEREDITH FOSTER,

IN BLESSED MEMORY

AND

WALTER CHRISTOPHER HOUGH

SON OF THEODORE AND HARRIET HOUGH

REQUEST THE HONOR OF YOUR PRESENCE

AT THEIR MARRIAGE

SATURDAY, THE EIGHTEENTH OF JUNE

TWO THOUSAND AND FOUR

AT SIX O'CLOCK

GREENACRES COUNTRY CLUB

SOMERSET, NEW JERSEY

One parent is deceased, remaining parent hosting, Version Two

MR. AND MRS. STUART FOSTER

AND

MR. AND MRS. THEODORE HOUGH

REQUEST THE HONOR OF YOUR PRESENCE

AT THE MARRIAGE OF THEIR CHILDREN

EMMA MARIE

AND

WALTER CHRISTOPHER

SATURDAY, THE EIGHTEENTH OF JUNE

TWO THOUSAND AND FOUR

AT SIX O'CLOCK

GREENACRES COUNTRY CLUB

SOMERSET, NEW JERSEY

Bride and groom parents co-hosting, Version One

MR. AND MRS. STUART FOSTER

AND MR. AND MRS. THEODORE HOUGH

WOULD BE HONORED

TO HAVE YOU SHARE IN THE JOY

OF THE MARRIAGE OF THEIR CHILDREN

EMMA MARIE

AND

WALTER CHRISTOPHER

SATURDAY, THE EIGHTEENTH OF JUNE

TWO THOUSAND AND FOUR

AT SIX O'CLOCK

GREENACRES COUNTRY CLUB

SOMERSET, NEW JERSEY

Bride and groom parents co-hosting, Version Two

MR. AND MRS. THEODORE HOUGH

REQUEST THE HONOR OF YOUR PRESENCE

AT THE MARRIAGE OF

EMMA MARIE FOSTER

TO

THEIR SON

WALTER CHRISTOPHER HOUGH

SATURDAY, THE EIGHTEENTH OF JUNE

TWO THOUSAND AND FOUR

AT SIX O'CLOCK

GREENACRES COUNTRY CLUB

SOMERSET, NEW JERSEY

Groom's parents hosting

MR. AND MRS. STUART FOSTER

REQUEST THE HONOR OF YOUR PRESENCE

AT THE MARRIAGE OF THEIR DAUGHTER

EMMA MARIE

TO

WALTER CHRISTOPHER HOUGH

SON OF

MR. AND MRS. THEODORE HOUGH

SATURDAY, THE EIGHTEENTH OF JUNE

TWO THOUSAND AND FOUR

AT SIX O'CLOCK

GREENACRES COUNTRY CLUB

SOMERSET, NEW JERSEY

Including groom's family

Modern

THE HONOR OF YOUR PRESENCE

IS REQUESTED

AT THE MARRIAGE OF

EMMA MARIE FOSTER

AND

WALTER CHRISTOPHER HOUGH

SATURDAY, THE EIGHTEENTH OF JUNE

TWO THOUSAND AND FOUR

AT SIX O'CLOCK

GREENACRES COUNTRY CLUB

SOMERSET, NEW JERSEY

Couple hosting, Version One

We ask only the dearest to our hearts

to join us in celebrating

the marriage of our daughter Emma

to

Walter Hough

Saturday, the eighteenth of June

Two thousand and four

at six o clock

Greenacres Country Club

Somerset, New Jersey

Jane and Stuart Foster

Bride's family hosting

EMMA FOSTER AND WALTER HOUGH

INVITE YOU TO SHARE WITH THEM

THE JOY OF THEIR MARRIAGE

SATURDAY, THE EIGHTEENTH OF JUNE

TWO THOUSAND AND FOUR

AT SIX O'CLOCK

GREENACRES COUNTRY CLUB

SOMERSET, NEW JERSEY

Couple hosting, Version Two

Mr. and Mrs. Stuart Foster

request the pleasure of your company

at a reception

in honor of

Mr. and Mrs. Walter and Emma Hough

Saturday, the eighteenth of June

Two thousand and four

at six o clock

Greenacres Country Club

Somerset, New Jersey

Belated reception

We invite you to join us
as we begin our new life together
on Saturday, June 18, 2004
at 6:00 pm
Greenacres Country Club
Somerset, New Jersey
Emma Foster and Walter Hough

Couple hosting, Version One

In light of the blessings
That we share on our wedding day
Please consider making your gift
A donation to the
Susan G. Komen Breast Cancer Institute
In honor of our marriage and
in loving memory of
Janice Weber

Thank you, Emma and Walter

Requesting no gifts, formal, separate card

Share in our happiness
as we get married
the eighteenth of June
at six o`clock
Greenacres Country Club
Somerset, New Jersey
Emma Foster and Walter Hough

Couple hosting, Version Two

a guide to printingpress by mountaincow

PrintingPress software combines features from many programs to make printing invitations at home with your PC and printer fast and easy. You can use the techniques in this book with any software to print your own invitations, but PrintingPress provides easy-to-use tools along with stylish fonts, graphics, and project samples that were specifically designed for home printing of invitations and personalized stationery.

The software is divided into three main sections: The Address Book stores all your names and addresses for use in your projects. The Mailing List lets you specify who is invited for each project, as well as keep track of who is coming, who is bringing additional guests, who sent what gifts, and who received a thank-you note. The Stationery includes all your cards and envelopes for the project and lets you design using photos, fonts, graphics, and more.

"I love this program PrintingPress from Mountaincow. It allows you to make your own wedding invitations on the computer."

Darcy Miller,
Editorial Director
Martha Stewart Weddings magazine

The Address Book

It doesn't have the same ring as "a little black book," but an electronic address book is much more practical. The PrintingPress Address Book holds all the contact information for your guests in one convenient place. This way, the addresses are available for birthdays, celebrations, and holiday cards year after year.

If you already have all your contacts in a computer database, whether it's with your email provider or in a spreadsheet, follow the instructions in the PrintingPress online help to convert your information to a CSV (comma separated value) file to import into your Address Book. If you're starting from scratch, simply choose *New Address* from the *Address Book* menu and type them in one at a time. After you type an address, click *Save and New* to save the contact information and clear the fields for the next address.

You will notice two special fields for inner and outer envelopes. If you are planning a wedding, these fields will be very useful. If you leave the label name fields blank, both the inner and outer envelopes, as well as the place cards, will be printed with the contact's first and last name. The label name field lets you enter a formal name for the addressed envelope, such as Mr. and Mrs. George Thomas Anderson. The inner envelope name field allows you to follow etiquette by specifying a different name for addressing inner envelopes, such as Mr. and Mrs. Anderson or Emma Renee and Guest.

"There is now a last minute alternative to email invitations and your computer's hokey graphic package. Print high-quality invitations on any kind of paper or envelopes from your own printer in less than 20 minutes."

Real Simple magazine,
August 2003

The Mailing List

You can create a customized mailing list for each project. If you are planning a wedding, for example, and you create a "save the date" project, you can select all of your out-of-town guests from your Address Book. Then you can create a shower invitation and create a new mailing list of just your girlfriends who are invited. For each separate list you can keep track of RSVPs, gifts received, and thank-you notes written. The Mailing List page is also where you will see your guest list at a glance, with a tally of who is attending, who isn't, and who still hasn't responded.

The Stationery

CARD LAYOUT, MARGINS, AND RIBBON HOLE GUIDES

When you start a new project, the first thing you can do is create your new stationery. Start with a card, click *Next*, and you will come to the layout window. Here, you can quickly and easily match the stationery on screen with the size of the stationery that you bought. You can specify any width and height you want—making it easy to work with odd-sized cards and envelopes—and you can choose one sided or two sided cards. You can select the number and orientation of folds, so the card can be a tent card or a greeting card. You can also set the number of cards to print on a single sheet if you want to cut the paper after you print.

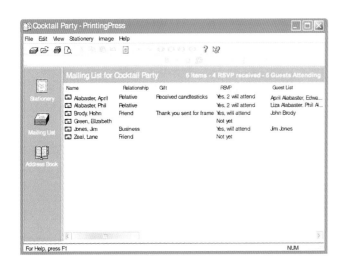

In the next window, you can set your margins to avoid typing over any preprinted designs on the card, such as graphics or borders. You can also customize the fold locations in case you want to be creative with semi-overlapping folds.

The next window creates ribbon hole guides. If you have ever printed a project with an overlay or embellishment, you know how hard it can be to get everything to line up properly. You can configure the ribbon hole guides to match the size and shape of your hole punch, and you can specify that they print horizontally for a ribbon embellishment or vertically for a program binding. You can also customize how far from the edge and how far apart they print.

MULTIPLE CARDS PER PAGE

To make folded cards from a letter-size sheet of paper, create a new project and create a new card. Use the dimensions $8\frac{1}{2}$" x $5\frac{1}{2}$" (21.6 x 14 cm) with one fold and two cards per page. If your cards have a vertical fold, they will print on top of each other and you can print them in the portrait orientation. If they have horizontal folds, they will be printed side by side and you must print them in the landscape orientation. When you are done, cut the page in half using a rotary cutter. These cards fit into an A2 envelope.

To make postcards, follow the previous instructions and choose no folds and four cards per page. Set the card size to $4\frac{1}{4}$" x $5\frac{1}{2}$" (10.8 x 14 cm), and decide if you want them horizontal or vertical. For horizontal postcards you must print them in the landscape orientation.

ENVELOPES

PrintingPress offers three envelope styles: Addressed, Reply, and Inner. The addressed envelope is the standard type of envelope you use with invitations. The reply envelope, most often used in wedding and Bar Mitzvah invitations, has the reply address on the front of the envelope. Reply envelopes are also great for designing personalized stationery because you can print a batch of the envelopes at a time. The trick is to put your return address on the back as well, and print "back only."

The inner envelope, most often used for formal occasions and weddings, will print only the guests' names (without their addresses). If the outside envelope reads Miss Emma Foster, the inner envelope will often read Miss Foster. According to etiquette, the inner envelope is also where the names of the invited children are listed.

Using the inner envelope feature is also ideal for the occasions in which you hand-deliver invitations and do not need to print an address, such as for school classmates or for neighbors for a block party.

PLACE CARDS

When a guest is marked in the Mailing List as attending, you can edit his or her information to include additional guests to create a place card accordingly. (This way, you won't waste time or paper on guests who are not coming.) PrintingPress allows flexible place card design to match the type of event you are having. Informal events can have just first names; more formal affairs can have a couple's full name and "You are seated at table..." printed on the inside. Hosts of business dinners can take advantage of putting names on both sides of the card so everyone at the table can learn one another's name or title.

Design Tools

IMAGES

To insert one of the built-in images onto a card, click the card and choose *Insert Image* from the *Image* menu. (Platinum users, this is located in the *Design* menu.) The *Image Browser* window lists the many graphics included with the software. Click the *Browse* button to look for any graphic or photo that is already on your computer. You can also copy a graphic or photo from another program by selecting *Copy* in the *Edit* menu. Then click a card and choose *Paste* from the *Edit* menu to insert the image. Platinum users can add images to envelopes and place cards as well.

Internet search engines provide a great way to find images. For example, visit www.yahoo.com, click the Images tab, and type the name of the image—for example, Easter egg—in the *Search Images* box. When you find an image, click the graphic to make it be displayed larger in the web browser, then right-click the large image and choose *Copy* from the pop-up menu. Open PrintingPress, click a card, and choose *Paste* from the *Edit* menu to insert the graphic into your card. Visit the Mountaincow website's Design Ideas section (www.mountaincow.com/design.html) for more suggestions on where to find graphics. Make sure you check copyright information before using anyone else's images for professional or business purposes.

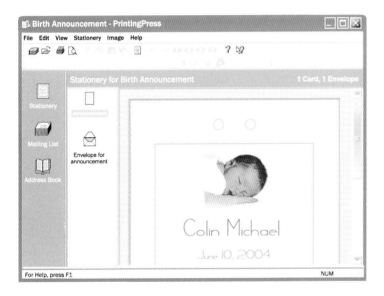

PHOTOS

Using photos in PrintingPress is easy. If you have a digital camera, follow the instructions that came with your camera for connecting the USB or memory card to your computer and copying the photos to a folder, such as the My Pictures folder. If you have prints and a scanner, follow your scanner software instructions to scan the photos into the same folder. You can also choose to have a photo CD created when you have your film developed; then you can import photos right from the CD. When you want to add the photo to a card, just choose *Insert Image* and click *Browse* as described in the previous section.

After you have imported your photo, you can use the PrintingPress tools—*Resize, Flip, Rotate,* and *Fade Image Border*—to adjust the photo. The *Fade Image Border* tool instantly blends the photo into the background of the card so you can make any picture look good on your stationery, no matter what is in the background of the photo.

PrintingPress also gives you the option of making your images transparent. This feature allows you to layer text or provide a more dramatic design for printing on vellum. To set the transparency of an image, select the image and choose *Image, Set Transparency.*

Another effect to apply to photos is to convert them to grayscale, which creates a black-and-white version of your image. Use this feature for a vintage style, especially when printing on vellum. To convert an image to grayscale, select the image and choose *Image, Convert to grays.*

BACKGROUND IMAGES AND BORDERS (PLATINUM ONLY)

Platinum users can add graphics and photos to envelopes and place cards, can make graphics and photos float over or behind text, and can even add borders to cards, envelopes, or photos. To add a graphic or photo to an envelope, click the envelope and choose *Image, Insert Image* from the *Design* menu. To add a background image, choose *Background Image, Add Background* from the *Design* menu. Background images are automatically set to be slightly smaller than the size of the card and to be semitransparent. You can adjust the transparency of the background image by selecting *Background Image, Set Transparency* in the *Design* menu. To make a graphic or photo float over text, choose *Image, Float Over Text* from the *Design* menu. To add a border to a card or envelope, click the card or envelope and choose *Stationery Border, Add Border* from the *Design* menu. To add a border to a photo or graphic, click the photo and choose *Image, Add Image Border* from the *Design* menu.

MONOGRAMS (PLATINUM ONLY)

A monogram can be made as simply as typing three initials. If you want to use a font outside of the built-in Flourish, Classic, and Modern styles, you can use any font and adjust the monogram by using the tool's advanced features. To show the advanced features of the Monogram tool, click the triangle to the left of *Show advanced controls*. After selecting the font, you can line up the three letters by their center, by the top of the letters, or by their baselines. The *Skew* feature adjusts the slant of the letters. By increasing the skew, any forward-slanting font will adjust to be more vertical.

To control how much the side letters extend to the center letter, increase or decrease the percentage of the overlap relative to the middle letter. You can also control the size ratio of the side letters to the center letter by increasing or decreasing the percentage. You can also customize the color of your monogram. Once you have created your monogram, you can resize it by selecting the monogram, then choosing *Monogram, Resize Monogram* in the *Design* menu.

TEXT BOXES (PLATINUM ONLY)

Text boxes give you the flexibility to move, overlap, and rotate text anywhere on the page and apply several design elements:

Align — Text boxes can horizontally justify text so it appears even on both sides. Text boxes also allow you to vertically align the text so it is aligned to the top, centered, or justified to the text box.

Condense/Expand — To squeeze or spread text to fit, use this feature to make adjustments vertically or horizontally.

Resize — The choice to Resize text box to fit text is set by default. This means no matter what you type, the text box adjusts to fit all the words. If you deselect this option, you can manually set the size of the text box, which is useful with justified text to increase the spacing between the letters.

FLOATING IMAGES (PLATINUM ONLY)

When you insert an image, you can choose *Float image over text.* This feature imports the image with handles on each corner so you can move it anywhere you like and change its size by clicking and dragging a handle. To keep the image in proportion, hold the Shift key while you drag a corner to make the image larger or smaller.

LAYERING (PLATINUM ONLY)

The moveable text boxes and images can be layered on top of one another for a more complex design. Select the text box and click the *Float over text* or *Float behind text* button in the Image toolbar for your desired design. To ensure the elements are in the correct order, select *Print Preview* in the *File* menu. The trick to creating white text on a colored background is to make the text not exactly white because text boxes automatically make all white transparent. Select a text box and choose *More colors* from the *Text Color* menu, then select white on the bottom-right corner. All of the values in the red, green, and blue fields will be 255. Change one of these to 254 to make the white text appear.

ALIGNMENT TOOLS (PLATINUM ONLY)

Found in the *Design* menu, the *Align* and *Distribute* tools allow you to align and distribute your floating objects. You can align the images relative to the stationery: centered or aligned at the top, bottom, left, or right. For example, if you want your text and an image to be exactly centered on a card, you can select both objects and choose *Align, Align Horizontal Center* in the *Design* menu.

If you want to space objects evenly, use the *Distribute* tools. For example, if you want objects be spaced with exactly the same amount of space between them horizontally, you can select the objects and choose *Distribute, Distribute Horizontally* in the *Design* menu.

If you want to give an alignment direction to all floating objects on the page, go to the *Edit* menu and choose *Select all floating images.* To just select a few floating objects, hold down the Shift key while clicking each desired object.

To make the images align or distribute relative to one another, deselect *Relative to stationery* in the *Design* menu.

RECOLORING IMAGES (PLATINUM ONLY)

By adjusting the hue and brightness of an image, you can completely change its coloring. To recolor an image, select the image and choose *Image, Recolor Image* in the *Design* menu. If you have a specific color in mind or want to match a text color, click *Match RGB.*

using your home printer

GETTING TO KNOW YOUR PRINTER

Whether you're printing your first PrintingPress project or your fiftieth, we always recommend doing a test print on scrap paper before using your stationery. If you're printing envelopes, draw a flap on one side so you'll know which direction to feed it. Printing can vary depending on the machine you use, and you'll want to make sure all your settings are correct.

First, determine if your printer is a **top-feed** where you place your paper in an upright position above the printer, like Epson, Canon or Lexmark printers, or a **bottom-feed** where your paper is laying in a tray below your printer, like an HP.

Next, know the difference between portrait and landscape orientation. If you were to design a sign where the top is $8\frac{1}{2}$" (21.6 cm) wide and the height is 11" (27.8 cm) tall, and then put a piece of paper in the printer, that is a portrait orientation.

If you want your sign to be 11" (27.8 cm) wide and $8\frac{1}{2}$" (21.6 cm) tall, you would need to print this as a landscape orientation since an 11 inch sheet won't fit in a standard printer without rotating it. When you rotate the paper, you tell the printer to rotate what you are printing by choosing *Landscape* in the *Print* window.

Some printers rotate clockwise (right) and others rotate counter-clockwise (left). To determine the direction of the landscape rotation, experiment by using a piece of paper that is 5" (12.7 cm) x 7" (17.8 cm). Set the *Landscape rotation* in the *Print* window to left rotation and see if it prints properly. If not, then your printer's landscape rotation is to the right.

THE BLEEDING EDGE

Most printers cannot print all the way to the edge of the paper. They have an unprintable margin area around the edge that is often as much as $\frac{1}{2}$ inch on bottom-feed printers. The ability to print all the way to the edge is called "borderless printing." Some photo printers can print borderless on standard photo sizes such as 3.5" x 5" (8.9 x 12.7 cm), 4" x 6" (10.2 x 15.2 cm), 5" x 7" (12.7 x17.8 cm), 8" x 10" (20.3 x 25.4 cm), 8.5" x 11" (21.6 x 27.9), and A4. A few can print borderless on any size card with varying degrees of success. Professionals typically print on a larger size card than they need which includes a "bleed" area that gets trimmed off after printing using a rotary cutter.

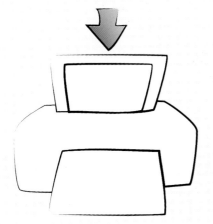

Top-feed printer

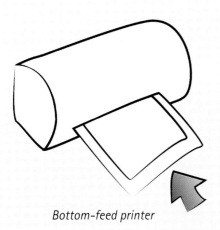

Bottom-feed printer

GENERAL TIPS FOR PRINTING

Keep it tall and wide. When printing on smaller pieces of paper and envelopes, the rollers that grip the paper work better when the paper is taller than it is wide. For this reason, even with top-feed printers it is best to feed smaller envelopes in landscape mode.

Know your load. Different printers have different bulk capacities, so be careful not to exceed yours. If you stack too many envelopes into the feed tray, your printer may have difficulty grabbing a single envelope and may feed several at a time. Bottom-feed printers tend to work better with at least five envelopes in the tray at a time. To avoid mis-feeds, keep it loaded.

Open up. Lined envelopes are thicker than unlined envelopes and will feed better if they are opened.

Through thick or thin. Many printers have a "thickness" or "envelope" switch that will allow thicker papers and envelopes to feed better. Older printers have a manual switch on the printer itself. Newer printers allow you to specify a paper type in the printer's *Properties* dialog.

Quality Counts. Experiment with the print quality settings in your printer's *Properties* dialog. You usually want a high quality, but sometimes it will put too much ink onto the paper and cause a bleed effect.

Vellum caveat. Only vellum specifically designed for an inkjet printer will yield positive printouts. Otherwise, a laser printer works best with vellum.

GETTING HELP

The *Help* menu in PrintingPress offers many ways to learn how to use the software. Begin with the *Online Tour*, which will open in a web browser and show you a graphical tutorial about how to use PrintingPress to design and print your invitations.

Start by opening a sample project to get some ideas. Choose *New Project* from the *File* menu select *Create New Project from a Sample Project* and then open a few of the projects to get ideas. Choose *Design Ideas* in the *Help* menu to view our newsletter projects. Use the CD enclosed in this book to view projects from the book.

Printing Envelopes
FOR A TOP-FEED PRINTER

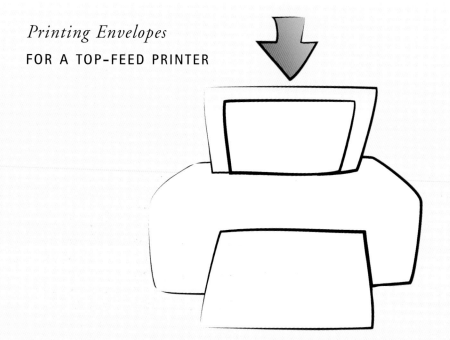

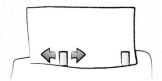

1. When you look at your top-feed printer, you'll see that there are adjustable guides within the input tray. These hold smaller pieces of paper straight as they're being fed into the printer. You'll notice that one of the guides can move to adjust to different paper and envelope sizes, whereas the other guide remains fixed and that the paper is aligned to the right side of the printer.

Once you have a project, use the *Stationery* view when designing and printing your cards and envelopes. Use the *Address Book* view for entering your names and addresses, and the *Mailing List* view for tracking RSVPs, gifts and guests. The names and addresses from your Mailing List will print on your addressed envelopes.

For additional reference choose *User Guide* in the *Help* menu and browse or search the help topics. You can print the topics if you prefer a printed manual for the software. If you get stuck, choose *Technical Support* from the *Help* menu to visit our website Technical Support Center for assistance.

BACKING UP

PrintingPress automatically saves your changes to its database, but just in case, you should periodically save a backup file to a removable disk. Select *Backup Project* from the *File* menu, and save it to your hard disk or a removable disk. As long as you back up your projects from time to time, you never need to worry

about a virus or other computer problem causing you to lose all of your hard work.

SHARING PROJECTS

Planning a big event such as a wedding, with numerous guest lists, a million details, and of course, lots of opinions, is often a group project. If everyone involved is using PrintingPress, joining forces is a breeze.

After a project is created, an invitation is designed, and a mailing list is made, the project can then easily be emailed to another person who also has PrintingPress for approval or additions. Go to the *File* menu, choose *Export project*, and save the project file to your hard drive. Then email the .pdf file to your family or friends as an attachment.

If you are the recipient of a .pef file, save the attachment to your hard drive. Open PrintingPress, go to the *File* menu, choose *Import project*, and browse for the file.

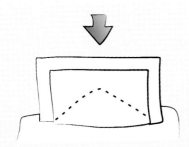

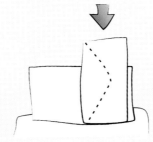

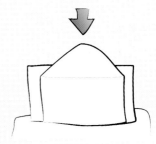

2. If the envelope width (measured holding envelope with the flap on top) is less than 8.5" wide, you can print the envelope portrait and feed the envelope with the flap closed, placing the top edge of the envelope into the printer first. To print the address, have the flap facing away from you. For the return address, have the flap facing towards you.

3. If the envelope is wider than 8.5" as with a #10 envelope or an outer envelope for a wedding invitation, you need to print in landscape mode. Be sure to feed the envelope with the flap closed, placing the left edge of the envelope into the printer first so that the envelope's flap is behind the envelope on the left side.

4. If you have PrintingPress Platinum, you are able to print the address on the front and the return address on the back in one pass as long as the envelope is less than 8 1/2" (21.6 cm) wide. To do so, open the envelope flap and feed with the bottom of the envelope first, making sure that the front of the envelope is facing you. Choose Print Front and Back in One Pass in the Print window.

Printing Envelopes

FOR A BOTTOM-FEED PRINTER

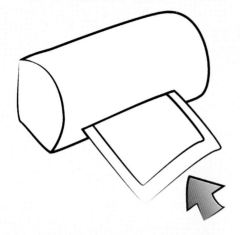

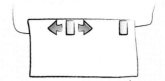

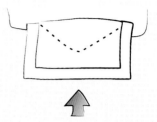

1. It's more difficult to access the movable paper guides on your bottom-feed printer, but once you find them you'll see that the movable guide is on the left and the paper is aligned to the right side of the printer. Because of the 'bent' paper path, envelopes tend to feed better and have fewer smudges when printed in landscape mode.

2. Generally, bottom-feed printers are fed with the side you want to print on face down. To print addresses, feed the envelopes with the flap facing up. To print the return address, feed the envelopes with the flap facing down. Please note that most laser printers require the paper to be fed face up.

If the other people involved don't have PrintingPress, you can still share the Mailing List to confirm addresses, titles, and spelling. When you choose *Export mailing* list from the *Mailing List* menu, it will be saved to your hard drive as a CSV file. Or choose *Print* from the *File* menu and print the Mailing List to give to relatives who are not online.

DOWNLOADING FONTS FROM THE INTERNET
Visit www.mountaincow.com/design.html for suggestions on where to find fonts to download from the Internet. Each font site has instructions on how to download and install the fonts. In general, you want to choose the TrueType version of the font.

Click the font file to begin the download and click Save to save it to a location on your computer, such as My Computer, Local Disk C:\. Then go to the font file you just saved, which may be in a compressed format, usually using WinZip—the font file's extension will be .zip. You must uncompress the font file in order to continue. Try double-clicking the Zip file to see you can extract the original. If you see a message that the file type is unknown, you may need to add WinZip to your computer. You can download

an evaluation copy of WinZip from www.winzip.com. Download and install WinZip, and then try extracting the font file again. Extract it to the same location, My Computer, Local Disk C:\.

After you extract the font file—or if it is uncompressed to begin with—it will have a .ttf extension for a TrueType font. Click the font file you want. Next, click the Windows Start menu and choose *Settings*, *Control Panel*, *Fonts* to open the Fonts folder. Click the *File* menu and choose *Install New Font*. Click the folder C:\ in the bottom-left corner of the *Install New Font* window. You will see your new font appear in the list at the top-left corner of of the window. Click your new font and click OK to install it. Repeat this procedure for as many new fonts as you want to add.

To see the new font in PrintingPress, click a card and select some text. Click the font selector in the toolbar and scroll to the new font's name and select it. The fonts are arranged alphabetically in the list and are displayed as they will print. On some versions of Windows you may need to close PrintingPress and open it again to see the new fonts you added.

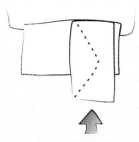

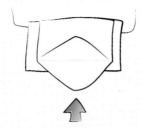

3. Feeding envelopes in the landscape mode varies from printer to printer. Some bottom-feed printers require the envelope flap to be on the left and some require it to be on the right. Test your printer to see which side is the "top" in landscape mode.

4. If you have PrintingPress Platinum, you are able to print both the address and the return address on the back in one pass as long as the envelope is less than 8 1/2" (21.6 cm) wide. The envelopes should be printed in portrait mode with the bottom of

the envelope fed first, the flap open and face down. Choose Portrait and Print Front and Back in One Pass in the Print window.

A Guide to the Bonus Content CD

This book comes with a bonus content CD that contains sample PrintingPress project files for all 35 projects in the book. It also contains five great invitation-style fonts, seventy five graphics, and over twenty borders for use with any software when creating invitations. The CD does not contain PrintingPress or PrintingPress Platinum software, but you can easily purchase the software from a wide selection of retailers or online at www.mountaincow.com.

index

about the authors

Patty Hoffman, director of communications at Mountaincow, has written about crafts, lifestyle, and entertaining for numerous magazines including *Seventeen, Family Circle,* and *Details.* Patty used PrintingPress to design every printed detail of her 2004 wedding. She holds a BA in journalism from Lehigh University.

Megan Eisen, CEO of Mountaincow, has created PrintingPress and many other software applications. She is an expert in graphic design and has created a wide variety of stationery and original fonts and graphics for invitations. Her stationery is featured in upscale stores such as Kate's Paperie in New York. She holds a BA from Stanford University.

Josh Eisen, president of Mountaincow, has created PrintingPress and many other software applications. He is an expert in the use of computer technology for custom invitation printing and advises stationery stores nationwide. He holds a BA and MBA from Stanford University.